THE ART OF
ORIENTAL COOKING

THE ART OF

ORIENTAL COOKING

BY MRS. JUNG SUCK CHOY

THE WARD RITCHIE PRESS

LOS ANGELES

DEDICATED TO

HENRIETTE LEHMAN

PREFACE

This cookbook contains carefully selected authentic recipes of Chinese, Japanese, and Korean dishes most of which will serve five to six persons. Almost all of the ingredients mentioned are available at your neighborhood grocery store.

Many years of experience as a housewife and teacher convinced me that Oriental cooking at home is an economical, time-saving, and enjoyable "art." Careful advance preparation is the secret of time-saving and good cooking; ingredients prepared early in the day can be cooked quickly at the last moment—most cooking requires not more than fifteen minutes. Methods of cutting vegetables and meat, decoration of the dinner table and dishes, and manner of proper serving have long been considered a fine art of Oriental cooking. (Eating with chopsticks adds a further artistic touch.)

Chinese food is the richest of the three; Japanese food is the sweetest; Korean dishes are between the two, not too rich and not too sweet. However, the basic ingredients required for all three kinds of cooking are more or less the same—white rice, vegetables, meats, and soy sauce. Styles of cutting, chopping, and slicing of ingredients are also the same. But the cooking methods and flavorings are a little different for each country, as the introduction for each country will explain.

There are interesting differences in eating customs: Japanese use only chopsticks and usually drink the last portion of their soup; Chinese and Koreans use both chopsticks and spoons, in accordance with the kind of dish served. In the Japanese tradition, all members of the family eat together on cushions at the one large lacquered dining table; the Chinese eat together at the dining table, sitting on chairs like Westerners. Traditionally, in Korea, individual dining tables were prepared for each person, and the dishes were eaten in separate rooms for male and female members of the family. Today, however, this custom has changed and all eat together at one large dining table sitting on the warm floor called On-dool.

All three countries have long recognized the importance of serving their foods attractively: garnishing is a part of the cooking art, because eye appeal is as important as taste appeal.

With many cookbooks available on Chinese, Japanese, and Korean dishes, it seems presumptuous to offer a new one. When I ventured to do this, nevertheless, it was the result of a "natural" process: I have given courses on Oriental cooking at the YWCA in San Francisco and in other places, have discovered which dishes my American friends like best, and have been asked for these recipes so many times that I thought I might as well write them down and make them generally available.

To Mr. and Mrs. Scott Fleming, who glued together my broken English, goes my deep gratitude. Without their assistance this book would never have been possible to complete.

I would also like to make special acknowledgment of the help given me by Mrs. Samuel V. Chamberlain, author of many excellent cookbooks, and Mrs. Helen Halmlund for their reading of my manuscript and valuable suggestions. I am grateful to my neighbor, Mrs. Kenneth A. Hayes, who first encouraged me to write this book and introduced me to Mrs. Chamberlain. My special thanks also go to Mr. Max Knight of the University of California Press, who has been editing my husband's manuscript on Political History of Korea, for his help and advice on my manuscript, especially his editing on introductions and historical backgrounds of the recipes.

I would also like to express my appreciation to all members of my cooking classes for their genuine interest in Oriental cooking and their kind cooperation in the classes. I am very grateful to Miss Ruth Olds for her voluntary typing and proofreading of these recipes and Miss Emily Huggins for her voluntary typing. My thanks also go to my daughter, Cora, for her assistance, and to my husband, who has been of constant aid in all steps of writing this book. Finally, I am particularly grateful to Henriette Lehman for her love and kindness for many years—without her love, I would never have been able to undertake this project and this book would never have been written.

MAY, 1964
BERKELEY, CALIFORNIA

MRS. JUNG SUCK CHOY

CONTENTS

INTRODUCTION

It is my pleasure and privilege to introduce THE ART OF ORIENTAL COOKING *to the American public. For many years I have known the author, Mrs. Jung Suck Choy, who studied in Korea, Japan and the United States. I met her and her family first in San Francisco while I was visiting the United States as a member of Education Mission sent by the American Military Government in Korea in 1946. Both Mr. and Mrs. Choy joined the faculty of Seoul National University in 1947—Mrs. Choy teaching home economics at the College of Education. Since 1950 in the United States she has been giving courses in Oriental Cooking at various social and church groups, including the YWCA and the Women's Society.*

On many occasions, Mrs. Chang and I have had the pleasure of visiting the Choy family, and we have enjoyed immensely Mrs. Choy's home cooking. THE ART OF ORIENTAL COOKING *is a combination of her personal experimentation through her years as a housewife and teacher and carefully selected authentic recipes of Korean, Chinese and Japanese dishes. She also adds a pinch of historical background and seasons her accounts with original stories about dishes—a recipe of cookbook-writing all her own. Thus, the book possesses a personality, which will surely be appreciated by Western housewives and the general public. To my knowledge Mrs. Choy's is the first authentic Oriental cookbook written by a competent scholar turned housewife, or housewife turned scholar, well acquainted with the Eastern-Western ways.*

DR. LEE WOOK CHANG
Former President of Seoul National University and Korean Ambassador to the United States.

THE ART OF
ORIENTAL COOKING

KOREAN FOOD

THE KOREAN PENINSULA is a land of 85,000 square miles of natural beauty—about the size of Minnesota. It has a population of 32 million, moderate climate, and four distinct seasons. Korea is an agricultural country: more than two-thirds of the people are farmers producing grains, vegetables, marine products, fruits, and meats. Korea is surrounded by the major powers of Asia—China, Russia, and Japan—and has many times been a battleground in the power struggle between them.

The Koreans are a peace-loving people; they have never attacked or invaded another country and have through the centuries preserved their customs, culture, language, and way of living. Above all, they are generous and hospitable to friends and strangers. When you get acquainted with a Korean he will usually ask you to his home for dinner. They enjoy eating and like good food. They developed their own cooking methods and many unique dishes such as *Sin Sul Lo*, "Angle Pot" (Eisenhower's favorite dish when he visited Seoul in 1952), *Bul Kogi* (barbecued beef), one of the most popular dishes during the 1962 World's Fair in Seattle, and *Kim Chee* (the Korean version of pickles).

Korea's capital has traditionally been the center for the development

3

of Korean cooking, because the royal and aristocratic families resided there. Women cooks (no professional cooks existed) prepared a large variety of dishes for their masters. Cooking in the royal palace was complex and time-consuming. Of the three meals, breakfast was considered the most important; guests were often invited for breakfast rather than for lunch or dinner.

Southern Korean food (except rice) is more salted and seasoned than Northern food because of the warm climate in the South. No refrigeration system existed, and salt was necessary to preserve meat. The main cooking utensils are: a large cooking pot for rice, a frying pan, and a charcoal broiler *(hwa ru)* for barbecue. Charcoal and firewood are the fuels used for cooking. Korean food is delicious. Those who know how to cook it will enjoy preparing it and serving it to family and guests.

Modern Korean cooking has been modified slightly from the old traditional methods as Western ingredients were introduced and accepted by Korean housewives who, however, jealously preserved the original native taste. The recipes in this book reflect this change. Every recipe has been tried many times by the author.

Rice, beef, pork, fish (fresh, dried, and salted), poultry, vegetables, and fresh fruits are the principal products in the Korean diet. Many Korean dishes are combinations of meats and vegetables. Koreans often use sprouts, leaves, roots, mosses, and seaweeds. Soy bean is an important part of the diet, used in the form of sprouts, oil, paste, and curd.

Sesame seed, pine nuts, soy sauce, bean paste, green onion, garlic, red pepper, sugar, honey, fresh ginger, black pepper, monosodium glutamate, sesame oil are the most common seasonings used in the vegetables, soup, and meat dishes. Toasted sesame seed is used for meat cookery or

4

as garnishing for broiled or barbecued meats. Crushed (blended) toasted sesames are also used for meat-and-vegetable combination seasoning.

Kim Chee is served at every meal. It is a popular pickle and consists of sliced turnip, green onion, red pepper, napa cabbage *(bai-chu)* and other vegetables. The ingredients vary somewhat at different times of the year. *Kim Chee* may be purchased in jars at some stores carrying Oriental foods.

Koreans often cook marinated meat and fish over a charcoal fire, especially during the summer. The winter favorite is a dish called *Sin Sul Lo*, named after the cooking pot used for its preparation. This is a cooker with a charcoal chimney in the center, and it is brought to the table for final cooking.

The Korean desserts are mainly fresh fruits and occasionally cooked dried persimmons, also date balls rolled in pine nuts or chestnut balls dipped in honey.

Korea does not produce tea, therefore Koreans commonly use rice "tea." After they have cooked rice, they transfer it from the pot, leaving 4 or 5 tablespoons of cooked rice in the pan, brown it over a flame to a golden dark brown, then pour water over the browned rice, and bring to a boil. They serve a bowl of rice tea during or after meals. Today Koreans also import and drink regular tea.

The food is served on a low table, sometimes on an individual table which is prepared in the kitchen and carried into the dining room, though today one large table is more common, so that members of a whole family can eat together. During the meal one sits on a soft cushion on the floor and enjoys the food.

SOUP (KOOK)

SOUP *is served at most meals. Every breakfast menu contains at least one kind of soup. Among the Oriental peoples the Koreans are the biggest soup eaters. Their soup bowl is twice the size of that of the Chinese and Japanese; it is usually made of brass or porcelain. The brass soup bowl is popular because it preserves heat, and Koreans like hot soup. It does not have a cover like the Japanese lacquer soup bowl. According to an old Korean custom, when you eat soup or other food it is permissible to make a "slurping" noise, which is taken to mean you consider the food delicious. Koreans eat soup with rice; sometimes they mix rice and soup and use brass or silver soup spoons with long handles.*

❦ BASIC CLEAR SOUP (KOOK)

½ pound lean beef
1 clove garlic, minced
2 green onions, finely chopped
1 teaspoon toasted, crushed
  sesame seeds (*see page 43*)
2 tablespoons soy sauce
1 tablespoon oil

4½ cups water or more
Salt to taste
Dash freshly ground
  black pepper
1 teaspoon monosodium
  glutamate

6

1. Cut meat into thin strips, then chop coarsely. Mix well with garlic, green onions, sesame seeds, and soy sauce.

2. Heat oil in soup pot. When oil is hot, put in seasoned meat and brown until juice comes from meat.

3. Now add 4½ cups water and bring to boil, then lower the flame and simmer for 20 minutes, until the meat is tender.

4. Add salt, pepper, and monosodium glutamate to taste. Serves 5-6 persons.

NOTE: This basic soup is a typical Korean dish and may have any type of vegetable or meat added to it—peas, mushrooms, cubed bean curd, egg, *wanja*, or *mandoo*. (*see page 50.*)

❧ EGG SOUP (KERAN KOOK)

A very light soup, wonderful to serve unexpected guests.

1 egg, slightly beaten
1 green onion, chopped crosswise
Mushrooms, canned or fresh sliced

1 can consommé, bouillon, or Korean basic clear soup
1 can water (measured in soup can)

1. Heat consommé and water to boiling point.

2. Put in mushrooms. (Don't boil, keep hot.)

3. Before serving, slowly add onions and pour beaten egg into hot soup, stirring gently and quickly to keep egg in shreds. (After egg is poured over soup turn off the heat.)

4. Serve immediately. Serves 5-6 persons.

NOTE: Fresh or frozen green peas may be substituted for green onions. Mushrooms are optional. Bean curd (*do-bu*) may be added. Use ¼ cake and cut into ½ inch cubes.

7

❦ VEGETABLE SOUP (YACHAI KOOK)

Beef soup bone (I recommend you save the bone from a chuck roast for this soup after using meat for BUL KOGI). *(see page 16.)*

1 bay leaf or 2 slices ginger	½ teaspoon monosodium glutamate
1 onion, halved	1 teaspoon salt

TO MAKE BROTH:

Cut all fat from bone and discard. Put bone in large pot, cover with water and add remaining ingredients. Bring to boil and simmer 1½ hours or more. Strain, cool, and skim off fat.

VEGETABLES:

½ dry onion, cut into large chunks	1 small bunch green onions, cut in 1 inch slices
1 large carrot, cut into quarters lengthwise, then slice crosswise on the diagonal, rotating carrot strip at each cut	2 or 3 stalks celery, sliced coarsely
	1 tomato, skinned and cut in chunks
2 zucchini, quarter lengthwise then slice	

This is a listing of suggested vegetables. You may use any leftover vegetables with good results, including cabbage, string beans, turnips, and others in equal amounts. Dry onions and carrots need to be added to simmering broth 5 to 7 minutes before other vegetables. Simmer all vegetables at least 15 minutes. Serves 5-6 persons.

SEASONING: Add five minutes before serving.

1 or 2 teaspoons soy sauce	Freshly ground pepper to taste
2 cloves garlic	½ teaspoon monosodium glutamate
Salt to taste	

FISH AND
SEA FOOD (HAISAN MUL)

KOREA, *like Japan, produces many delicious marine products, as the peninsula is mostly surrounded by the sea. Yet there are not many fish dishes.* GUI KUI *(baked individual crab dish) is one of my own recipes which I developed from an experience twelve years ago when I visited Seoul. My husband and I were invited for dinner to Dr. Han Chi-jin's home along with an American missionary, the late Dr. Fisher, who for years had taught at Chosun Christian College (now Yun See University). We enjoyed all the dishes Mrs. Han prepared but I liked the crab-meat dish best. I decided to experiment on a recipe based on crab meat. When I came back to the United States in 1948, I tried a simple crab dish on my American friends in Seattle and found that they liked it. Next time, I added a few more ingredients to the original one, introduced it to members of the Japanese church, and, again, they liked it. I gained confidence, named it* GUI KUI, *which means baked crab dish. I was very pleased to hear Mr. and Mrs. Ward Ritchie say "superb" when I had the pleasure of serving it to them at my home.*

Besides GUI KUI, *I introduced other fish dishes which became popular with members of my YWCA cooking classes in San Francisco. Some of the dishes can be served as hors d'oeuvre.*

9

❧BAKED INDIVIDUAL CRAB DISH (GUI KUI)

1 cup cooked crab meat or canned, flaked

½ pound fresh bean sprouts, or canned

½ dry onion, finely chopped

1 or 2 green onions, chopped

5 water chestnuts, finely chopped

3 or 4 eggs, depending on size

1 teaspoon cornstarch

2 teaspoons monosodium glutamate

Salt and dash of pepper to taste

Toasted sesame seeds (for garnishing) (*see page 43*)

SAUCE:

1 cup water or stock

1 tablespoon cornstarch

1 teaspoon sugar

1 teaspoon monosodium glutamate

2 teaspoons soy sauce

Dash of salt and pepper to taste

1. Bring 1 cup of water to boil. Add fresh bean sprouts and boil 2-3 minutes. If using canned bean sprouts, drain well before using.

2. Chop bean sprouts, onions, and water chestnuts, finely; mix together with crab meat.

3. Stir eggs together, but do not beat. Add to crab and vegetables, then mix.

4. Add seasonings and mix very slightly. Over-mixing at this stage will make it watery.

5. Spoon mixture into six greased baking shells or individual casseroles.

6. Bake in a hot oven 400° for about 25-30 minutes, until golden brown.

7. Mix sauce ingredients together in small saucepan, cook over medium heat, stirring constantly until thickened.

8. Just before serving, top each shell with 2 tablespoons sauce and sprinkle toasted sesame seeds over the top. Serve immediately. Serves 5-6 persons.

❧ CRAB DISH (GUI JIM)

1 large cooked crab. Ask butcher to clean and crack
1 tablespoon oil
1 clove garlic, minced

2 or 3 slices ginger, shredded or minced
1 small dried onion, sliced thin

SAUCE:

1 tablespoon flour
½ cup water
1 teaspoon curry powder (optional)

1 teaspoon monosodium glutamate
Garnish with green onions or green pepper

1. Heat frypan, put in oil, and sauté garlic and ginger.

2. Add dried onion. Do not brown.

3. Put meat from crab in frypan and cook about 2-3 minutes. Do not use high heat. Mix flour, water, curry powder, monosodium glutamate and pour over crab. Cook until gravy is thick. Garnish and serve immediately with cooked rice. Serves 5-6 persons.

❧ FRIED FISH (SANGSUHN JUHN)

1 pound boned white fish (rock cod recommended)
1 teaspoon salt
Dash of pepper

4 tablespoons flour, or less
2 eggs slightly beaten
5 tablespoons salad or cooking oil

1. Clean and cut fish in squares or strips.

2. Lightly sprinkle salt and pepper on each side and let stand at least 20-30 minutes (better flavor).

3. Roll each piece in flour and then dip into beaten egg and fry in a small amount of oil (enough to prevent sticking). Fry until golden brown or tender. Serve hot or cold.

4. Serve with any of sauces on *page 21*. Serves 5-6 persons.

❧ DEEP FRIED FISH WITH SWEET AND SOUR SAUCE (SANGSUHN JIM)

2 or 3 pounds white fish   Salt

BATTER:

1 cup water   1 teaspoon ginger root juice
1 egg   (optional)
1 cup flour

1. Wash and clean fish, drain well and then cut into serving pieces about 4 inches long.

2. Slash the edges of the fish so that it won't curl up during frying; then lightly sprinkle salt on both sides. Let stand about 10-15 minutes.

3. Mix batter ingredients gently. Dip fish in batter and fry in deep fat on both sides until light brown or until done.

SWEET AND SOUR SAUCE:

½ pound bean sprouts   1 teaspoon soy sauce or more
1 carrot, thinly shredded   ½ teaspoon monosodium glutamate
2 Oriental mushrooms, sliced   1 tablespoon sugar
2 or 3 green onions, chopped   1 garlic, minced
1 tablespoon cornstarch   1 slice ginger root, minced
1 cup water   ¼ cup vinegar, or less

1. Fry bean sprouts, carrot, mushrooms, green onions in little amount of oil, stirring frequently and set aside. This should be for a few minutes only.

2. Mix cornstarch, water, soy sauce, monosodium glutamate, sugar, garlic, ginger and vinegar. Cook until thick, stirring constantly.

3. Add fried vegetables to sweet and sour sauce and pour over fish. Serves 5-6 persons.

NOTE: Bamboo shoots may be added, if desired.

❦ SALMON WITH BEAN CURD (SANGSUHN DUBU JIM)

6 pieces sliced salmon	2 tablespoons soy sauce
Salt	1 teaspoon monosodium glutamate
Cornstarch	½ tablespoon fresh ginger, sliced
1 tablespoon oil	(or ⅛ teaspoon powder)
½ to 1 cup water	2 tablespoons wine
1 tablespoon sugar	1 bean curd (*do-bu*)

GARNISH:

2 or 3 green onions, sliced	2 red peppers or Tabasco sauce (optional)

1. Salt salmon lightly on both sides and let stand about 10 minutes.

2. Dust with cornstarch. Heat ¾ tablespoon oil for frying. Cook thoroughly. Remove salmon. Discard oil from pan.

3. In frying pan put ½ to 1 cup water or soup stock and bring to boil. Add: 1 tablespoon sugar, 2 tablespoons soy sauce, 1 teaspoon monosodium glutamate, ½ tablespoon sliced ginger or powdered ginger. When brought to a boil add 2 tablespoons wine.

13

4. Add 1 bean curd cut in 1 inch pieces (never cover pan containing bean curd as it makes it tough). Let boil to heat through.

5. Place fish on top of bean curd. Garnish with sliced ginger and sliced green onions. Spoon sauce over the fish to mix flavors.

6. Optional: 2 or 3 red peppers or a little Tabasco sauce. Serves 5-6 persons.

MEAT DISHES

BARBECUE (BUL KOGI)

KOREA *has well developed barbecue cooking. The method is about the same as in the United States—the use of charcoal and a grill on an open-fire pit. Barbecued short ribs and beef have been the most popular dishes. Since the Korean war there are many barbecue restaurants in Japan, especially in Tokyo, managed by Koreans, and we hear that they are doing well. I found that my American friends like Korean barbecue dishes, and they are easy to prepare. In order to give them authentic Korean flavor charcoal should be used. It is Korean custom to eat barbecued short ribs with your hands. Have plenty of napkins on hand and eat the ribs while they are hot. We speak of "do it yourself barbecue", because everybody can have the meat as he likes it—rare, medium, or well done. Korean barbecue can be done indoors or outside. If you do your barbecuing inside, use the fireplace to prevent smoke.*

❧ BASIC KOREAN BARBECUE MARINADE

This marinade is intended for use on meats to be charcoal broiled. It may be used for whole or sliced beef, chicken, pork, beef heart, pheasant, wild duck, etc.

15

2 teaspoons sesame seed oil or any
type salad oil
1 teaspoon brown sugar
2 green onions, finely chopped
2 tablespoons toasted sesame seeds
2 cloves garlic, minced fine

4 tablespoons soy sauce or more
½ teaspoon monosodium glutamate
1 tablespoon dry sherry (or other
cooking wine)
Dash of black pepper

Combine and mix well.

❧ KOREAN BARBECUED BEEF (BUL KOGI)

THIS CHARCOAL BROILED STEAK *is very delicious and very famous in Korea. It can be prepared from prime rib, sirloin, top round or chuck steak. My favorite is the chuck, as it has superior flavor and is quite tender when properly cut into narrow strips. Also it is the most economical. If using sirloin, you may wish to leave the steak whole. Top round steak may be either cut into serving size pieces, or cut into the narrow strips in the same manner as the chuck.*

INGREDIENTS:
About two pounds of steak, or whole chuck roast, well marbled with fat.

MARINADE:
4 tablespoons soy sauce (less if
desired)
2 tablespoons sesame oil or salad
oil
2 tablespoons brown sugar
½ teaspoon honey
1 thin slice fresh ginger, minced
(optional)

1 or 2 green onions, finely chopped
1 or 2 cloves garlic, minced
2 tablespoons sesame seeds, toasted
1 teaspoon monosodium glutamate
1 tablespoon sherry
Dash freshly ground black
pepper

16

1. Cut steak into serving size pieces or into narrow strips about ¼ inch by 4 inches, always cutting strips across the grain for tenderness.

2. Combine marinade ingredients, add meat pieces, mix thoroughly. Marinate meat strips 15 to 30 minutes. Larger serving pieces should be marinated 1 to 2 hours.

3. For best results, broil over hot charcoal. Turn meat only once—thin strips should cook in 2 or 3 minutes. Steaks will take longer, of course. Cooking time depends on degree of doneness desired. Serves 5-6 persons.

NOTE: This can be cooked under stove broiler, or can be quickly pan fried in a hot frying pan with a small amount of oil. This method will not have the flavor as when charcoal broiled.

❧ BARBECUED SHORT RIBS (KAHLBI KUI)

2 pounds short ribs, lean and
   meaty

1 tablespoon brown sugar
Salt

MARINADE:

4 tablespoons soy sauce
1 tablespoon sherry
1 tablespoon cooking oil
1 tablespoon brown sugar
2 cloves garlic, minced

1 thin slice fresh ginger, minced
1 green onion, chopped fine
2 teaspoons toasted sesame seeds
   Dash of pepper
½ teaspoon monosodium glutamate

1. Trim fat from ribs. Very thick ribs may be split in half to insure tenderizing by marinade.

2. Lay ribs flat, bone down on cutting board. Using a sharp knife, score deeply lengthwise and crosswise, cutting about every ½ inch, and about

½ inch deep. Score sides of ribs in same manner except the back. Cut once along the bone on the back lengthwise with the point of a sharp knife. This will aid in separating meat from bone easily after cooking.

3. Sprinkle ribs lightly with salt. Rub brown sugar on ribs, using only one tablespoon sugar for 2 pounds of ribs, and rubbing thoroughly into cuts. Let stand 1 to 2 hours to tenderize.

4. Combine marinade ingredients. Add ribs. Mix well and let stand 30 minutes to 1 hour.

5. Broil over charcoal 5 to 7 minutes. These may be oven broiled but will be less tasty. In oven, broil a few minutes longer.

6. Eat with fingers. Serves 4 persons.

NOTE: Koreans save these bones after meat is eaten and boil in one quart of water, salt, and monosodium glutamate for about 1½ hours. This makes a good soup stock.

❧ BARBECUED GROUND BEEF

1 pound ground chuck or lean beef
2 or 3 stalks green onions, chopped
2 cloves garlic, minced
2 teaspoons brown sugar
2 tablespoons soy sauce
1 teaspoon monosodium glutamate

⅛ teaspoon pepper
1 or 2 slices ginger, minced
1 teaspoon sesame seeds
1 teaspoon to 1 tablespoon sesame oil

1. Mix ingredients thoroughly.

2. Shape meat into square patties and score lightly with knife.

3. Brush meat with a little sesame oil and broil to desired doneness on hibachi. Serves 5-6 persons.

❧ BARBECUED SKEWERED BEEF (SAHN JUHK)

½ pound chuck roast or other
  lean beef
1 bunch green onions or 2 dry
  onions

¼ pound medium size fresh
  mushrooms
Oil

MARINADE:

2 tablespoons soy sauce
1 teaspoon oil
1 tablespoon sherry
1 teaspoon sugar

1 clove garlic, minced
2 teaspoons toasted sesame seeds
1 teaspoon monosodium glutamate

1. Cut beef into 1½ inch cubes.

2. Cut green onions into pieces slightly longer than meat cubes or quarter the dry onions.

3. Wash medium size whole mushrooms with salt water.

4. Combine marinade ingredients. Add meat; marinate 15 to 30 minutes.

5. Run the skewers through a cube of meat, onion, and mushrooms. Repeat once to have six pieces on each skewer. Either metal or bamboo skewers can be used.

6. Brush lightly with oil to retain juices, then broil over charcoal or oven broil, basting with the marinade two or three times. Broil 5 to 7 minutes, until desired doneness. Serves 5-6 persons.

❧ FRIED BEEF (KOGI JUHN)

1 pound tenderloin beef or top
round steak
1 teaspoon salt
Dash of pepper

4 tablespoons flour
2 or 3 eggs, lightly beaten
5 tablespoons oil

1. Cut steak into 2 inch wide strips. Lay strips on cutting board long-side forward. Slice diagonally making very thin pieces about ⅛ inch thick. Most pieces will be about 2 inches by 2 inches by ⅛ inch. This takes practice before you can cut uniformly even pieces.

2. Hit both sides of thin beef slices with cutting edge of knife, *bruising* meat but not cutting fibers (as in Swiss steak). This will prevent shrinking and shortens cooking time.

3. Sprinkle both sides of each piece with salt and pepper and set aside for at least 30 minutes.

4. Roll both sides of beef slices in flour very lightly, then dip into beaten egg.

5. Pan fry in small amount of salad oil over medium heat until golden brown on both sides.

6. Serve hot or cold. If uniform size is desired, cut into 1 inch squares for hors d'oeuvre, or 2 inch squares for dinner entrée.

7. Serve with any of the sauces on *page 21*. Serves 5-6 persons.

NOTE: If this dish is prepared in advance and you wish to serve it hot, you may reheat in a covered casserole in a 325° oven for 7 to 10 minutes.

☙ SAUCES AND DIPS

1. VINEGAR-SOY SAUCE (CHO-CHANG SAUCE)

¼ cup soy sauce
1 teaspoon vinegar
½ teaspoon sugar
½ teaspoon monosodium glutamate

1 green onion, chopped fine
1 clove garlic, minced
1 tablespoon chopped peanuts
(optional)

Mix together and serve as a dip for mandoo, fried fish or fried meat.

2. ¼ teaspoon prepared mustard
2 tablespoons soy sauce

½ teaspoon sugar

Mix all ingredients together.

3. 2 tablespoons tomato catsup
Few drops of Tabasco sauce

1 to 2 tablespoons horseradish
1 tablespoon lemon juice

Combine and mix well.

4. 2 tablespoons soy sauce
1 tablespoon vinegar
½ teaspoon sugar

Chopped green onions (only
white part)
Dash of paprika and cayenne

Mix well.

☙ FRIED GROUND BEEF (WANJA JUHN)

1 pound ground chuck
2 tablespoons soy sauce
1 teaspoon salt
Dash of pepper
½ teaspoon monosodium glutamate
1 tablespoon toasted sesame seeds

2 cloves garlic, minced
2 green onions, finely chopped
½ cup flour
2 or 3 eggs, slightly beaten
4 tablespoons oil

1. Mix together ground chuck, soy sauce, salt, pepper, monosodium glutamate, sesame seeds, garlic and onions.

2. Shape into round flat patties about 2 or 3 inches in diameter.

3. Roll in flour very lightly, then dip into the egg which has been slightly beaten.

4. Fry patties, a few at a time, in enough oil to prevent sticking, until golden brown. Add more oil as needed.

5. These can be served either hot or cold, with meatball sauce. (*see page 21 for sauce recipe.*) Serves 5-6 persons.

❧ MEATBALLS (WANJA)

1 pound ground chuck or lean beef	1 teaspoon monosodium glutamate
½ cake bean curd, or 2 tablespoons bread crumbs	2 tablespoons sesame seeds, toasted
2 or 3 green onions, finely chopped	4 tablespoons pine nuts (optional)
2 tablespoons soy sauce	4 tablespoons flour
½ teaspoon brown sugar	1 egg, slightly beaten
Dash of pepper	4 tablespoons oil for frying

1. Mix by hand first eight ingredients. Shape this mixture into small balls about walnut size for hors d'oeuvre. For entrées you may double the size. If you use pine nuts, enclose 2 pine nuts in each ball.

2. Roll each ball in flour lightly, then dip into slightly beaten egg and deep fry until brown at 365°, or you may pan fry these in ¼ inch oil at medium temperature.

3. Meatballs may be made ahead of time; then before serving preheat oven to 325° and heat in a casserole for about 10 minutes.

4. Serve hors d'oeuvre with Korean sauce of your choice, *page 21*.

5. If serving meatballs as entrée, add Korean gravy.

SAUCE OR GRAVY:

1 cup water or stock
1 tablespoon cornstarch
1 teaspoon sugar
1 teaspoon monosodium glutamate

2 teaspoons soy sauce
1 tablespoon sherry (optional)
Dash of salt and pepper to taste

Mix sauce ingredients together in small saucepan, cook over medium heat, stirring constantly, until thick. Serves 5-6 persons.

NOTE: If using *wok*, or frypan, heat about 1 ½ cups oil over medium hot flame. Place six meatballs at a time in the hot oil. Cook short time until brown. These can be sautéed with fairly good results.

❦ BOILED RIBS WITH VEGETABLES (KAHLBI JIM)

2 to 3 pounds short ribs
2 tablespoons brown sugar
1 carrot
4 or 5 mushrooms
1 tablespoon oil
2 dry onions, sliced into rings
1 small can (4 oz.) water chestnuts

2 cloves garlic, minced
Dash of black pepper
1 teaspoon monosodium glutamate
¼ cup or ½ cup soy sauce
¾ cup water, or less
2 tablespoons pine nuts
1 green onion
2 tablespoons toasted sesame seeds

1. Trim fat from ribs. Very thick ribs may be split in half. Score deeply every ½ inch on both sides of short ribs.

2. Rub sugar on ribs using only one tablespoon sugar for 2 or 3 pounds of ribs.

23

3. Wash, peel, and cut carrot in pieces 1 inch long.

4. Slice mushrooms. (If using Oriental mushrooms, soak in warm water at least 15 minutes before using.)

5. Brown ribs on both sides in 1 tablespoon oil.

6. Add onions, carrot, water chestnuts, mushrooms, and all combined seasonings and pour over the meat; add water and cook until tender.

7. Just before serving, arrange on a plate and decorate the top with pine nuts, shredded green onion, and toasted sesame seeds. Serves 4-5 persons.

❧ BEEF AND VEGETABLES BAKED IN SEA SHELLS (KOGI WA YACHAI CHOKEE KUI)

1 pound ground chuck beef
2 or 3 green onions, finely chopped
1 or 2 stalks celery, diagonally sliced
1 dry onion, chopped
½ pound fresh cooked bean sprouts, coarsely chopped

1 can water chestnuts, sliced (4 oz. size)
2 Oriental mushrooms (optional)
1 or 2 tablespoons pine nuts
1 or 2 tablespoons flour
3 or 4 eggs

SEASONING:

1 clove garlic, minced
1 teaspoon sugar
1 teaspoon monosodium glutamate
1 thin slice fresh ginger, grated
2 or 3 drops Worcestershire sauce

⅛ teaspoon cinnamon powder
Salt and pepper to taste
1 tablespoon sesame seeds (toasted) for garnishing

1. Mix thoroughly with ground beef, green onions, celery, dry onion, cooked bean sprouts, water chestnuts, mushrooms, and pine nuts. Mix in flour and seasonings.

24

2. Add eggs one at a time and mix gently (do not beat).

3. Put mixture into six greased baking sea shells or individual casseroles; brush top with egg yolk.

4. Bake in a hot oven 400° for about 20 to 25 minutes, until golden brown.

5. Serve immediately with sauce and sesame seeds. Serves 5-6 persons.

SAUCE:

1 tablespoon cornstarch	1 teaspoon sugar
1 cup water or stock	1 teaspoon monosodium glutamate
2 teaspoons soy sauce	1 tablespoon wine
1 tablespoon tomato catsup	1 teaspoon ginger juice (optional)

1. Mix all ingredients together in a small saucepan; cook over medium heat, stirring constantly until thick.

❦ BARBECUED SPARERIBS AND BOILED SPARERIBS (DOEJI KAHLBI KUI AND POKKUM)

Almost all Korean farmers raise pigs either for domestic meat supply or to be sold at the market. Pigs can be raised cheaply from left-over food or from soy beans. Korean pork is delicious because the pigs are not too fat and the meat is very tender. The following two recipes are especially designed for American friends.

❦ BARBECUED SPARERIBS DELUXE (DOEJI KAHLBI KUI)

3 to 4 pounds spareribs, lean and meaty	1 teaspoon salt
	Dash of pepper

NOTE: Have butcher crack ribs so they may be cut in half. A whole rib is too awkward to handle with fingers.

½ cup soy sauce
2 tablespoons brown sugar
1 tablespoon tomato catsup
2 cloves garlic, minced
1 teaspoon monosodium glutamate

1 teaspoon or 1 slice freshly
  grated ginger
2 teaspoons toasted sesame seeds
1 green onion, chopped

1. Trim off fat from spareribs and sprinkle with salt and pepper on both sides. Let stand for at least 10 to 15 minutes or longer.

2. Preheat oven to 375°. Put spareribs lengthwise on rack of broiling pan.

3. Bake spareribs on meaty side first for about 30 minutes, then turn to other side and bake for 15 minutes.

4. Brush one side of ribs with barbecue sauce and bake for 5 to 7 minutes. Then turn and brush other side and let bake for 5 to 7 minutes.

5. Before serving sprinkle both sides of ribs with sesame seeds.

6. Serve hot or cold with cooked rice. Serves 5-6 persons.

❦ BOILED SPARERIBS WITH SOY SAUCE (DOEJI KAHLBI POKKUM)

2 to 3 pounds meaty pork spareribs
  cut in desired size pieces
¼ cup soy sauce
1 tablespoon brown sugar
1 clove garlic, minced

Dash of pepper
1 teaspoon monosodium glutamate
1 slice fresh ginger, grated
1 tablespoon tomato catsup
1 onion, sliced

GARNISH:
Whole sesame seeds toasted and one green onion chopped

1. Trim off excess fat on each piece of sparerib and parboil for 15 minutes.

2. Combine soy sauce, brown sugar, garlic, pepper, monosodium glutamate, fresh ginger, and tomato catsup.

3. Marinate spareribs in combined sauce for 10 to 15 minutes.

4. Preheat *wok* or frypan and brown ribs on both sides, mixing once or twice while cooking. Add sliced onion and simmer for 45 minutes to 1 hour, until fork-tender.

5. Before serving, garnish with toasted sesame seeds and green onion.

6. Serve with cooked rice and green salad. Serves 5-6 persons.

NOTE: 1 small can of pineapple chunks or water chestnuts can be added to the spareribs before serving.

❧ PORK CHOPS WITH SAUCE (DOEJI KOGI JIM)

4 to 6 medium thick pork chops   Salt or seasoning salt

SAUCE:

1 to 1½ cups water   ¼ cup water
¼ can bamboo shoots   2 tablespoons brown sugar
2 or 3 mushrooms (dried) or   1 tablespoon or more soy sauce
  ¼ lb. fresh   1 teaspoon monosodium glutamate
1 radish (Oriental) or turnip,   1 clove garlic, minced
  sliced   1 or 2 slices (or more)
2 teaspoons cornstarch   ginger shredded

GARNISH:

Green onion chopped, or sliced green pepper rings

1. Trim off as much fat from meat as possible. Sprinkle lightly with salt. Fry without oil on both sides until golden brown.

2. Remove from pan.

3. In same pan, add bamboo shoots, mushrooms, and radish with 1 to 1½ cups of water and bring to a boil. Mix cornstarch with ¼ cup water, brown sugar, soy sauce, monosodium glutamate and stir into pan, adding rest of sauce ingredients. This will make a thin gravy.

4. Put the pork chops in the sauce and let it boil again and serve immediately. Garnish with either green pepper rings or green onion. Serves 5-6 persons.

CHICKEN DISHES

CHICKEN *is an important domestic animal for Korean families, especially for farmers. They supply not only meat and eggs for the farmers all year round, but are also timekeepers, rousing the farmers early in the morning. During spring, summer, and winter, Koreans let the chickens run around all day to find their food until the sun sets. In the evening they return home for additional food usually given by old grandma or grandpa who anxiously await their return and know their exact number. During the most part of autumn the chickens are placed in the chicken houses to prevent them from eating up the harvest grains in the fields. It is very common when you are invited for dinner by farmer friends to be offered chicken.*

The last chicken recipe, Chicken Rolls, is my own design when I taught Home Economics courses at the Teacher's College of Seoul National University in 1947 and 1948. I introduced the chicken roll dish to my students and found they liked it. Ever since then, when I invite American friends for dinner I usually prepare it and receive favorable comments. I am glad to see that Mrs. Samuel V. Chamberlain, author of many excellent cookbooks, included my chicken rolls recipe in her book, THE CHAMBERLAIN CALENDAR OF AMERICAN COOKING. *I hope you will experiment with the chicken rolls on your friends, although rolls take much time to prepare.*

❦ CHICKEN DELUXE WITH THICK GRAVY (TAHK JIM)

1 stewing chicken, cut into
   serving pieces
2 teaspoons salt
5 to 6 cups water
2 slices fresh ginger root (optional)
1 teaspoon monosodium glutamate

½ cup mushrooms, sliced fresh
   or canned
½ cup water chestnuts, sliced
2 green onions, finely chopped
   Salt and pepper to taste

GRAVY INGREDIENTS:

½ cup flour
2 teaspoons sugar
4 tablespoons soy sauce

2 cloves garlic, minced
2 tablespoons toasted sesame seeds
   Small amount cold water

1. Place chicken in a deep heavy saucepan with enough water to cover, add 2 teaspoons salt and ginger and monosodium glutamate; cook slowly at simmer until partially done, about 1½ hours.

2. Remove the chicken from the liquid (broth). Combine all ingredients for gravy: flour, sugar, soy sauce, garlic, sesame seeds, and water, and mix until smooth. Pour gravy into hot broth, stirring constantly.

3. Add mushrooms, water chestnuts, and mix thoroughly and bring to a boil. Add dash of pepper, taste for salt and add more if needed. When gravy starts to thicken put in the chicken and green onions and mix gently. Cook another 2 minutes.

4. Serve with cooked hot rice. Serves 5-6 persons.

NOTE: Stewing chicken takes longer to cook. Frying chicken takes half the time. If you like plain chicken and gravy, omit mushrooms and water chestnuts.

❧ CHICKEN WITH SWEET SOUR SAUCE (TAHK JIM)

2-to-3-pound frying chicken,
  cut into serving pieces
2 tablespoons wine
1 tablespoon soy sauce

1 teaspoon salt
1 egg
3 to 4 tablespoons cornstarch
  Oil for deep frying

SAUCE:

1 cup soup stock or water
2 to 3 dried mushrooms or ¼ lb.
  fresh, sliced thin
¼ can bamboo shoots, sliced thin
1 clove garlic, minced

1 tablespoon cornstarch
1 tablespoon sherry
1 tablespoon brown sugar
1 teaspoon monosodium glutamate
2 teaspoons soy sauce

GARNISH:

Chopped green onions and sesame seeds

1. Clean chicken and drain well. Combine wine, soy sauce, egg, salt, and cornstarch.

2. Marinate chicken in the sauce for at least 30 minutes. Drain.

3. Heat oil in deep frypan (electric frypan 365°). Fry several chicken pieces at a time until golden brown. (Fry twice for best results.)

SAUCE:

1. Put water or soup in saucepan. Add mushrooms and bamboo shoots and cook until tender, about 5 to 7 minutes.

2. Mix other ingredients, adding a little water to make a paste to pour over mushrooms, bamboo shoots and soup, stirring constantly until medium thick.

3. Pour sauce over chicken and garnish with green onions and toasted sesame seeds. Serves 5-6 persons.

❧ CHICKEN WITH VEGETABLES (TAHK POKKUM NO. 1)

3-pound frying chicken, cut into
   serving pieces
1 small can pineapple chunks
½ cup pineapple juice from can
  1 tablespoon (or less) fresh ginger,
   grated
  2 cloves garlic, minced

2 tablespoons soy sauce or more
¼ cup oil
¼ pound fresh mushrooms, sliced
  in half
2 or 3 green onions, diagonally
  sliced
1 teaspoon toasted sesame seeds

1. Mix together pineapple chunks, juice, ginger, garlic, and soy sauce. Pour this mixture over the chicken and let it marinate 3-4 hours, turning the pieces once or twice. If you do not like a strong ginger taste, then you might use only one large slice of ginger, grated.

2. Drain the chicken, reserving the marinade, and in a skillet brown the pieces on all sides in ¼ cup of hot oil.

3. Remove the chicken to casserole and discard the oil remaining in the skillet.

4. Pour the reserved marinade over the chicken, sliced mushrooms, and green onion, cook it uncovered in a 325° oven for about 45 minutes or until tender, basting once or twice. Garnish with toasted sesame seeds before serving.

5. Serve with cooked rice. Serves 5-6 persons.

❧ CHICKEN IN SOY SAUCE (TAHK POKKUM NO. 2)

2½-to-3-pound frying chicken,
   cut into serving pieces
  1 medium dry onion
¼ pound fresh mushrooms sliced,
  or 1 small can mushrooms

1 teaspoon toasted sesame seeds
  or toasted almonds (garnish)
1 green onion, chopped

MARINADE:

2 tablespoons soy sauce	½ teaspoon monosodium
1 tablespoon oil	glutamate
1 teaspoon brown sugar	Dash of pepper
1 garlic, minced	⅛ teaspoon salt

1. Clean chicken and wipe thoroughly. Cut into serving pieces, leg and thigh separated, breast cut into 4 pieces. Use gizzard and liver if desired.

2. Mix marinade ingredients in saucepan, add chicken pieces, and let stand together at least 30 minutes.

3. Slice onion lengthwise, top to bottom; slice mushrooms, add to chicken.

4. Cover pan and bring to boil. Reduce heat to low and cook about 30 to 35 minutes or until meat is tender, turning meat occasionally.

5. Before serving, garnish with green onion and either sesame seeds or almonds. Serves 5-6 persons.

❧ BARBECUED CHICKEN (TAHK KUI)

1 frying chicken, cut in serving pieces	1 teaspoon salt
	1 tablespoon oil

BASTING SAUCE:

½ cup soy sauce	1 teaspoon fresh ginger, grated
1 to 2 tablespoons brown sugar	1 teaspoon monosodium glutamate
1 tablespoon sherry	1 tablespoon whole toasted sesame
1 or 2 cloves garlic, minced	seeds (for garnishing)

1. Clean the chicken and slightly sprinkle salt on both sides; let stand for at least 20 to 30 minutes.

33

2. Preheat broiler and put the chicken into broil pan meaty side up, brush with oil.

3. Broil about 30 minutes, then turn and broil about 15 minutes.

4. Combine all basting sauce ingredients and brush bone side with marinade; broil 5 minutes.

5. Turn meaty side and brush other side gently with basting sauce and broil for another 5 minutes.

6. Before serving, sprinkle with whole toasted sesame seeds.

7. Serve either hot or cold. Serves 4 persons.

❧ CHICKEN ROLLS (TAHK KEERAN MARI)

EGG SKINS:

3 eggs
1 tablespoon cornstarch

2 tablespoons water

FILLING:

2 raw chicken breasts, sliced and chopped

1 or 2 stalks green onion, chopped
½ onion, minced

SEASONING:

1 tablespoon Worcestershire sauce
2 tablespoons soy sauce, or less
3 tablespoons cooking wine

1 teaspoon salt
2 tablespoons cornstarch
1 teaspoon monosodium glutamate

1. Grease a hot 8 inch skillet with about 1 teaspoon of oil. Pour about 2 or 3 tablespoons egg mixture into skillet, spread over bottom.

2. Fry over medium heat until egg mixture shrinks from the side of the skillet.

3. Turn skin and fry for 1 minute on the other side.

4. Remove carefully and cool. Repeat as above until batter is used up.

5. Mix seasoning and chicken together and wrap in skins. Steam chicken rolls about 10 minutes and then fry until golden brown.

6. Serve with sauce if desired, but they are already seasoned and sauce is optional. Serves 5-6 persons.

SAUCE:

2 tablespoons soy sauce	1 teaspoon sugar
1 teaspoon ginger juice	1 teaspoon tomato catsup
1 tablespoon lemon juice or vinegar	

❦ EGG GARNISH

Many Korean dishes use this egg garnish.

2 eggs	¼ teaspoon sugar
Dash of salt and white pepper	Very small amount of oil

1. Combine eggs, salt, pepper, and sugar. Beat until well mixed. This is easily done using a pair of pointed chopsticks for beating.

2. Pour a half teaspoon or less of oil into a 6 or 8 inch frying pan, spread over bottom with paper towel. Warm pan over low heat.

3. Pour half of egg mixture, or less, into pan. Spread it thinly and evenly over bottom of pan by tipping pan to each side, then cook over low heat until set. Remove from pan in one piece as a pancake. Repeat process until egg mixture is used up. Then cool.

4. Roll egg pancakes and cut into very thin strips. Separate with fingers. Sprinkle over top of dishes as a garnish or for decoration.

VEGETABLES AND SALADS

PRACTICALLY ALL THE VEGETABLES *that you find in the United States grow in Korea. Combinations of vegetables and meats make common dishes, prepared with a variety of seasonings, such as sesame seeds, soy sauce, green onions, garlic, and dash of red pepper. Most vegetables are grown in the flat fields, but some of them are found in the hills. During the spring, teen-age girls and boys in the village usually hunt around for mountain-grown (sometimes called "natural") vegetables. Many stories and songs have been written about the vegetable-hunting teen-agers. The following song is typical:*

> White blue-bells, white blue-bells,
> In deep mountains, dark valleys, where I can find my blue-bells?
> When I found a few,
> They overflowed my bamboo basket,
> Eh-heh-ya, eh-heh-ya, eh-heh-ya,
> Eh-hehra, nan-da, you pretty blue-bells,
> You are taking my heart, my heart, blue-bells.

*Thus, here is the song of a girl's pure heart, dreaming of love even if she fails to dig up blue-bells (*TORAJI*).*

*Since the blue-bell roots are not available in this country, the blue-bell recipe is not included here; instead, I designed a Korean-American salad in addition to the three original Korean vegetable (*NAMOOL*) dishes.*

36

❧ KOREAN-AMERICAN COMBINED SALAD (NAMOOL)

½ pound fresh bean sprouts
1 or 2 carrots
½ cucumber (optional in season)
1 tablespoon raisins
¼ pound cooked meat (chicken,
ham, shrimp or crab meat)

2 tablespoons mayonnaise or salad
dressing
½ teaspoon lemon juice
⅛ teaspoon dry mustard
1 tablespoon toasted sesame seeds
Egg garnish (*see page 35*)

1. Put fresh bean sprouts in rapidly boiling water, bring to boil again, and boil for 2 minutes only. Drain and cool. Gently press out water with hands.

2. Peel carrots, thinly slice diagonally. This can be done easily with a potato peeler; then slice the diagonal rounds into thin shred-like strips. Salt lightly and let stand 10 minutes.

3. Slice cucumber thinly, do not peel if skin is tender.

4. Wash raisins in hot water and drain well.

5. Dice meat into ½ inch cubes.

6. Mix mayonnaise, lemon juice, and dry mustard.

7. Mix all vegetables and meat and toss in bowl gently with dressing.

8. Garnish with egg and toasted sesame seeds. Serve in large salad bowl or in individual dishes. Serve immediately to preserve crispness. Serves 5-6 persons.

NOTE: If you wish to serve an authentic Korean salad, omit mayonnaise and substitute 1 tablespoon of soy sauce and 1 teaspoon of sesame oil.

❧ CUCUMBER WITH MEAT SALAD (OI NAMOOL)

¼ pound lean beef
1 tablespoon soy sauce
1 clove garlic, minced
1 teaspoon sugar or less
1 teaspoon sesame oil or cooking oil
1 teaspoon toasted sesame seeds
1 teaspoon monosodium glutamate
2 medium cucumbers
 Salt

1. Cut any type of lean beef into thin strips across the grain. Mix with soy sauce, garlic, sugar, oil, sesame seeds, and monosodium glutamate. Fry in hot pan about 2 minutes. Set aside.

2. Peel cucumbers only if skin is tough. Slice thinly. Sprinkle lightly with salt and let set for 5 minutes.

3. Squeeze liquid out of cucumbers between the palms of the hands and add to the meat. Fry another two minutes and serve hot. Serves 5-6 persons.

NOTE: If desired, sprinkle with a little bit of cayenne before serving.

❧ SPINACH WITH MEAT (SHIKUMCHI NAMOOL NO. 1)

1 bunch spinach
1 teaspoon salt
½ pound lean beef, chopped finely, not ground
1 tablespoon toasted crushed sesame seeds
1 teaspoon cooking or salad oil
2 teaspoons sugar
1 clove garlic, minced
1 green onion, chopped
½ tablespoon soy sauce
 Salt
 Dash of cayenne pepper
1 teaspoon monosodium glutamate

1. Cut off roots and wash spinach very thoroughly.

38

2. Boil about one cup of water, then add spinach and salt, cook about 2 or 3 minutes. Do not overcook. Keep bright green.

3. Drain and press out the water with hands. Cut in 2-inch lengths.

4. Fry meat, adding garlic, onion, soy sauce, oil, sugar and monosodium glutamate. Also add sesame seeds, reserving about 1 teaspoon for garnish. Mix all ingredients well.

5. Mix meat with the spinach and season with salt and dash of cayenne pepper to taste.

6. Serve hot or cold. Garnish top of spinach with remainder of sesame seeds. Serves 5-6 persons.

NOTE: Prepare in same way without meat and use 2 teaspoons vinegar. This is very good. Serve cold in summertime.

❧ SPINACH SALAD (SHIKUMCHI NAMOOL NO. 2)

1 bunch fresh spinach   1 cup of water
  Salt

SEASONINGS:

2 teaspoons soy sauce   1 clove garlic, minced
½ teaspoon sugar   2 teaspoons sesame seeds
1 green onion, chopped   1 teaspoon oil
  Dash of salt, black pepper,   1 teaspoon monosodium glutamate
  paprika

1. Wash and clean spinach thoroughly.

2. Bring water to boil; add 1 teaspoon salt (this keeps vegetables green).

3. Add spinach to boiling water; cook 2 to 3 minutes. Do not overcook.

4. Drain well and do not wash.

5. After cool, cut into 2-to-3-inch strips and press out excess water.
6. Combine all seasoning ingredients and toss with spinach gently.
7. Garnish with sesame seeds; serve on attractive dish. Serves 5-6 persons.

NOTE: This may be served winter or summer. If you desire vinegar, add 2 teaspoons before serving because vinegar tends to discolor the green. Serves 5-6 persons.

❧ GREEN BEANS (KEEN KONG NAMOOL)

1 pound green beans or 1 pkg. frozen French cut green beans
1 tablespoon cooking oil
¼ pound meat (pork or beef) thinly sliced
1 onion, thinly sliced
½ cup mushrooms, sliced
1 clove garlic, minced

1 tablespoon soy sauce
Dash of salt and pepper
1 teaspoon sugar
½ teaspoon monosodium glutamate
1 teaspoon toasted crushed sesame seeds
¼ cup water
Toasted almonds (optional)

1. Wash, drain, and "string" beans on both sides. Slice thin lengthwise of bean, if thick; cut into ½ lengths.
2. Preheat large frying pan, add oil, and sauté meat for about 2 minutes for beef, 5 minutes or more for pork.
3. Add onion and cook only until tender, not brown.
4. Add fresh beans or defrosted frozen ones and mushrooms, and stir-fry a minute. Then add water, soy sauce, salt, sugar, pepper, monosodium glutamate, garlic and sesame seeds. Cover with lid and cook until beans are tender, about 5 to 7 minutes. Do not overcook.
5. Garnish with toasted almonds, if desired. Serves 5-6 persons.

❧ COOKED RADISH WITH MEAT SALAD (MU NAMOOL)

1 radish sliced diagonally, then shredded (can be purchased at either a Chinese or Japanese grocery store)

¼ pound beef tenderloin cut in thin strips

1 clove garlic, minced

1 piece fresh ginger, minced (optional)

2 teaspoons soy sauce

2 teaspoons brown sugar

1 teaspoon sesame oil or salad oil

1 teaspoon monosodium glutamate

Dash of black pepper

1 green onion, chopped

1 uncooked egg

1. Marinate beef in garlic, ginger, soy sauce, brown sugar, sesame oil, monosodium glutamate, black pepper and green onion.
2. Fry beef without oil until tender. Add radish and cook about 10 minutes (until radish is cooked). While cooking, stir two or three times.
3. Just before serving, add egg to middle of pan and cook until half done, then mix quickly with other ingredients in pan. Serve immediately. Serves 5-6 persons.

❧ FRIED WATER CRESS WITH MEAT (MINARI JUHN)

2 bunches water cress

¼ pound beef

2 or 3 green onions

3 eggs

¼ cup flour or more

2 tablespoons water

1 teaspoon monosodium glutamate

Salt to taste

Dash of black pepper

1. Cut water cress into 2-inch lengths. Wash thoroughly and drain well.
2. Slice beef in thin strips; chop green onions.
3. Mix water cress, beef, onions. Add eggs, flour, and water and mix gently. Season last.

4. Drop two tablespoons of mixture on oiled skillet which has been heated slowly (just like a pancake).

5. Fry until brown, then turn and brown other side.

6. Serve immediately with *Cho-Chang* sauce. (*see page 21.*) Serves 5-6 persons.

NOTE: The water cress should be very fresh. Do not overcook.

❧FRIED SQUASH (HOBAHK JUHN) NO. 1

2 or 3 medium zucchini	2 eggs, beaten
Salt	4 tablespoons oil for frying
4 tablespoons flour	

1. Slice squash diagonally about 1/4-inch thick. Sprinkle with a very little amount of salt.

2. Roll each slice in flour lightly, then dip into beaten egg. Fry only a few squash at a time in hot frying pan in a small amount of oil, frying both sides until golden brown. Remove from pan as soon as fork-tender. Do not cook until limp. Add a bit more oil for each batch.

3. Serve with soy sauce (*Cho-Chang*). (*see page 21.*) Serves 5-6 persons.

NOTE: Try this same method of cooking for other vegetables, such as sweet potatoes, egg plant, white potatoes, green peppers, carrots or string beans.

❧FRIED SQUASH (HOBAHK JUHN) NO. 2

2 or 3 summer squash	2 or 3 eggs
1/4 pound ground chuck	4 tablespoons flour
2 or 3 green onions, chopped	

| 1 teaspoon salt | Dash of black pepper |
| 1 teaspoon monosodium glutamate | Oil for frying |

1. Wash and slice the squash diagonally; then shred. Mix the squash with ground chuck and chopped green onions.

2. Add the eggs one at a time; mix gently; gradually mix the flour together with them, and then the seasoning.

3. Heat a little amount of oil in the frypan, then pour 1 heaping tablespoon of squash and meat mixture; fry slowly until golden brown (they should look like pancakes).

4. Serve hot or cold with *Cho-Chang* sauce. (*see page 21.*) Serves 5-6 persons.

❧ TOASTED SESAME SEEDS

| 1 cup white sesame seeds | 1 teaspoon salt |

1. Put sesame seeds into a heavy skillet. Place over a medium flame, stirring constantly, and brown slowly. When seeds are browned, remove from fire. An electric skillet is perfect for this as the heat is easily controlled and even. Set control at 350°.

2. Take out toasted seeds you wish to use for vegetables and add salt; mash until pulverized. You can easily do this in a blender.

3. Store in clean, dry, covered jars. They will not spoil.

NOTE: Toasted sesame seeds are used whole as a meat garnish or for marinades. The toasted seed are usually crushed for use in vegetable dishes or salads.

SPECIAL NATIONAL DISHES

❧ SIN SUL LO (ANGLE POT DISH)

SIN SUL LO *is Eisenhower's favorite Korean dish. Its origin goes back to the Koguryo period (37 B.C.-668 A.D.), when it was prepared in the royal palace by the female cooks. It is a complex and time-consuming dish in terms of materials and preparation.* SIN SUL LO *means "Angle Pot Dish." It is a winter favorite, cooked and served at the table, formerly a festival dish used at New Year's Day, weddings, anniversaries, etc. Now the dish has been much simplified and is easy to make, and most Korean families have a* SIN SUL LO *cooking pot in their homes. You can have* SIN SUL LO *almost any time at any first-class Korean restaurant. As you can see in the San Francisco De Young Museum, the Koguryo* SIN SUL LO *pot was first made of clay, later of brass or silver. The brass* SIN SUL LO *pot is practical because you don't have to clean it as often. It is easy to find in Korean, Chinese, Japanese, or some of the American department stores.*

The SIN SUL LO *recipe calls for layers of turnips, seasoned beef strips, shellfish, sliced chicken breasts, and deep-fried* WANJA *balls, all simmered together in a broth at the last moment. I first present the "company version" of* SIN SUL LO *and afterward two types of simple family style* SIN SUL LO *recipes. (Use an electric frying pan if you don't have a* SIN SUL LO *pot.)*

❧ FESTIVAL VERSION OF SIN SUL LO

¼ pound beef tenderloin

(Seasoning for Beef):

  1 teaspoon soy sauce
½ teaspoon sugar

½ pound scallops
½ pound prawns
½ plump chicken breast

(Wanja [Meatball] Ingredients):

½ pound ground beef
¼ cube bean curd cake *(do-bu)*
  1 green onion, minced
  2 teaspoons toasted sesame seeds
  1 egg beaten
  2 tablespoons flour
    Oil for frying

GARNISH:

  2 tablespoons pine nuts
  1 tablespoon pimiento, sliced
   (optional)

1 clove garlic, minced
  Dash of salt and pepper

2 medium turnips or ½ *dai-kon*
  (Oriental radish) if available
½ teaspoon salt
1 teaspoon sugar

1 clove garlic, minced
½ teaspoon soy sauce
1 teaspoon sugar
  Dash of salt and pepper
2 or 3 cups broth. (Use clear beef
  or chicken broth seasoned to
  taste, or canned consommé
  soup.)

2 green onions, thinly sliced
  including tops

45

1. Wash and peel *moo* (or turnips). Cut in half lengthwise, then slice thinly crosswise. Place in a saucepan with 1 cup cold water, ½ teaspoon salt, and 1 teaspoon sugar. Boil covered for 5 minutes.

2. Slice beef into thin 1-inch strips, then mix well with "seasoning for beef" (soy sauce, sugar, garlic, salt and pepper).

3. Break scallops in half, do not cut.

4. Shell and devein prawns, wash, drain, and cut in half crosswise.

5. Skin and debone chicken breast. Slice meat thin.

6. Combine *wanja* ingredients (ground beef, *do-bu*, green onions, garlic, sesame seeds, soy sauce, sugar, salt and pepper). Form into miniature meatballs, smaller than walnuts. Roll in flour, then dip in beaten egg, and fry in hot deep fat.

7. Arrange ingredients in *Sin Sul Lo* or frying pan in following order:
   1st layer—*dai-kon* or turnip slices
   2nd layer—seasoned beef strips
   3rd layer—halved scallops
   4th layer—prawns
   5th layer—chicken strips

   On top, place meatballs around the chimney of the *Sin Sul Lo*, using about one dozen, or scatter about in frying pan.

8. Garnish with pine nuts, pimiento, and green onions.

9. Gently pour 1 or 1½ cups hot broth over all. Cover and bring to boil. At this time, bring the bubbling *Sin Sul Lo* dish to the table. Serve immediately in individual bowls. Add more broth to *Sin Sul Lo* as necessary. Serves 4-5 persons.

❧ SIMPLE SIN SUL LO NO. 1

½ pound beef sirloin
½ to 1 pound raw shrimps
1 piece raw chicken breast
1 cake bean curd *(do-bu)*
5 dry mushrooms or ¼ pound
   fresh mushrooms

5 leaves Chinese cabbage, or
   ½ bunch spinach leaves, or
1 Japanese *dai-kon* or
1 pound turnips
1 can chicken broth or consommé
1 tablespoon monosodium
   glutamate
Salt and pepper to taste

GARNISH:

Egg garnish
Pine nuts

Sliced green onions

1. Slice beef tenderloin very thin across grain. Peel and devein raw shrimps. Skin and bone chicken. Slice into very thin strips.

2. Cut bean curd into 2-inch cubes.

3. For dry mushrooms, soak in warm water for about 10-15 minutes. Slice mushrooms into strips or quarter fresh mushrooms.

4. Wash Chinese cabbage or spinach and drain. Cut diagonally into 2-inch strips, or quarter and then thin slice the *dai-kon* or turnips.

5. Arrange ingredients in *Sin Sul Lo* or frypan in following order:
   1st layer—Chinese cabbage, spinach or turnips
   2nd layer—mushrooms
   3rd layer—bean curd
   4th layer—beef

47

5th layer—shrimp
6th layer—chicken

Garnish top with egg, pine nuts, and green onions.

6. Gently pour hot consomme or chicken broth over all the ingredients. Cover and bring to boil. Cook until meat is tender, 5 to 10 minutes after bringing the ingredients to a boil.

7. Serve immediately in individual bowls. Add more broth to *Sin Sul Lo* as necessary. Serves 5-6 persons.

NOTE: Any meat (scallops, pork, etc.) can be substituted in place of chicken, beef or shrimp.

SAUCE FOR DIPPING (mix together):

¼ cup crushed sesame seeds	2 tablespoons soy sauce
1 teaspoon sugar	Dash of pepper
½ teaspoon monosodium glutamate	Salt to taste
½ to 1 cup water	2 or 3 drops Tabasco sauce

This sauce is used for dipping the ingredients of *Sin Sul Lo*.

❦ SIMPLE SIN SUL LO NO. 2

6 leaves Chinese cabbage	¼ to ½ pound raw shrimps
1 recipe of fried fish (*see page 11*)	¼ pound scallops (raw)
1 dry onion, diced	1 can Gingko nuts (6½ oz. can)
1 bean curd, cut in squares	1 bunch green onions
4 or 5 dried Oriental mushrooms (soaked)	2 cans bouillon or consommé
	1 tablespoon sherry

48

Arrange ingredients in the *Sin Sul Lo* in the following order:

1st layer—Chinese cabbage

2nd layer—fried fish cut in squares

3rd layer—dry onion, bean curd, mushrooms

4th layer—shrimps

5th layer—scallops, broken into smaller pieces

Top layer—garnish with fried fish squares, Gingko nuts, green onions cut in 1-inch lengths.

1. Prepare bouillon or consommé according to directions on can and heat to boiling point, then add 1 tablespoon sherry at last minute.

2. Pour bouillon or consommé over the above layers in the *Sin Sul Lo* and cook 5 to 10 minutes after the liquid has come to a boil.

3. Serve with sauce below. Serves 4-5 persons.

SAUCE:

2 tablespoons lime juice	1 stalk green onion, chopped
2 teaspoons dry mustard, to which a little hot water and soy sauce is added	½ teaspoon monosodium glutamate
	1 teaspoon sugar
3 tablespoons soy sauce	Sesame seeds

Mix above ingredients together.

NOTE: After *Sin Sul Lo* has been served, there will be left over broth in the *Sin Sul Lo*. Bean threads can be cooked in this broth and served as an additional dish.

❦ MANDOO (KOREAN DUMPLINGS WITH MEAT BALLS INSIDE)

MANDOO *is the Korean version of "Ravioli" and resembles Chinese* GOW JEE *(transparent dumplings), but it is a more complicated dish than* GOW JEE, *and it needs more skill to make the right shape of* MANDOO. *A Korean proverb says: "If you make a good shape of* MANDOO, *a lovely girl baby will be born to you." A little patience and practice are required to make good* MANDOO. *It is an ideal side dish together with rice and* KIM CHEE *when you have company. It would seem that once you know how to make* MANDOO *and have tasted it, you won't be able to resist having more of it. Mrs. Herzberger, who is East Indian and one of my students, married to a philosophy professor, tells me that she makes* MANDOO *at least once a week and eats them for breakfast as well as for lunch and dinner. This is also the favorite dish of my daughter, who is majoring in Home Economics. She likes fried* MANDOO *best.*

MANDOO *may be eaten as hors d'oeuvre deep fat fried, boiled in a soup, or steamed as a side dish at dinner. This recipe will make 60 to 80* MANDOO. *They may be frozen and kept for use at a later date.*

1 pound *won-ton* skins (may be either round or square)

FILLING:

1 pound ground chuck or ground lean pork	1 egg
1 can sauerkraut	1 tablespoon oil (omit if using pork)
1 cake *do-bu* (bean curd cake)	2 teaspoons cornstarch
1 pound bean sprouts	1 teaspoon sugar
4 green onions, chopped finely	⅛ teaspoon ginger powder, or cinnamon powder (optional)
1 clove garlic, minced	

50

2 teaspoons salt	2 teaspoons monosodium
⅛ teaspoon pepper	glutamate
Dash paprika	1 tablespoon toasted sesame seeds

1. If using pork, pan fry before mixing with other ingredients.

2. Chop sauerkraut coarsely. Wrap in clean dish towel or cheesecloth and squeeze out moisture as much as possible.

3. Wrap bean curd in cloth and squeeze it until all moisture is removed. Add to sauerkraut.

4. If using fresh bean sprouts, add them to 1 cup boiling water, bring again to boil, and boil for 2 minutes. Drain and rinse to cool. Chop coarsely, squeeze out moisture in same manner, and add to above. If using canned bean sprouts do not cook, just drain and squeeze.

5. Add all remaining ingredients of filling and mix very well.

6. If you use round *won-ton* skins place one spoonful of filling on the lower half of the circle of dough, dampen edge of upper half and pinch edges together securely. These will look like turnovers and are easier to make than the square *won-ton* skins.

7. Place the square *won-ton* skin in the left hand with a corner facing you. Put a tablespoon of *mandoo* filling in center mounded high—do not spread out. Wet two upper edges and fold up lower half, pressing edges together. Place left thumb in middle of bottom of triangle, fold left corner over back of thumb, then bring right corner around and lap over left side, first dampening one side so they will stick together. This takes practice before you can manage to have everything hold together. The finished shape should look something like this:

51

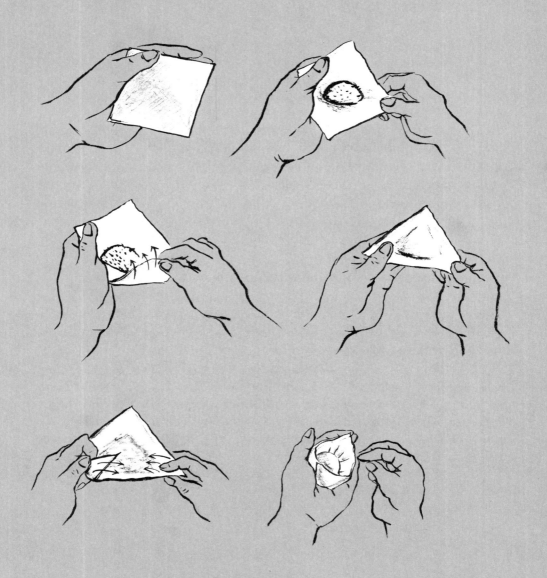

8. For hors d'oeuvre, deep fat fry the *Mandoo* in oil heated to 350°. Put in 5 *Mandoo* at a time and fry 3 minutes or less until a golden brown in color. Serve with *Cho-Chang* sauce (*see page 21*).

9. For soup add *Mandoo* to basic Korean clear soup on *page 6*. Boil about 5 minutes until the *Mandoo* floats to the surface, bottom up. This indicates the *Mandoo* is cooked through and ready to serve. Garnish with green onion and egg.

10. *Mandoo* may also be cooked by boiling or steaming 15 to 20 minutes and served as a dinner dish with *Cho-Chang* sauce. Serves 8-10 persons.

❧ MANDOO PII (MANDOO SKIN)

There is much work to making MANDOO PII, *and most Koreans in this country prefer to buy* WON-TON *skins and reduce the time in making* MANDOO. *However you might be interested in trying to make the skin for yourself. So I have included this recipe for the adventurous.*

2 cups flour	1 egg white
¾ cup water	1 teaspoon salt

1. Mix together and make a stiff dough. Turn dough onto a lightly floured surface and let stand for 5 minutes.

2. Knead 7 to 10 minutes until dough is smooth. Roll out to ⅛-inch thickness and cut with large round biscuit cutter or slice into 2-inch squares.

NOTE: Any leftover *Mandoo Pii* can be cut into strips and deep fat fried until golden brown and served in the same manner as potato chips.

❧ JUHN KOL (MEAT AND VEGETABLE DISH)

This dish closely resembles Japanese SUKIYAKI *and is cooked at the table.*

1 pound trimmed beef tenderloin, cut in very thin slices. If possible ask your butcher to *sukiyaki* cut it for you.

MARINADE FOR MEAT:

¼ to 1 cup soy sauce
2 tablespoons sugar
1 tablespoon oil
1 tablespoon toasted crushed sesame seeds

1 clove garlic, minced
1 or 2 green onions, chopped
Dash pepper

1 bean curd cake *(do-bu)*
2 dry onions, thinly sliced lengthwise
1 white radish
½ cup mushrooms, sliced (Oriental)
½ pound fresh bean sprouts
2 cups celery, thinly sliced diagonally

1 bunch watercress, *bok choy* or Chinese cabbage (optional)
1 bouillon cube in 1 cup water
2 tablespoons pine nuts (optional)
1 to 2 tablespoons oil for frying
2 or 3 eggs

1. Slice beef into very thin slices, or have butcher slice it for you.

2. Mix marinade ingredients, add the meat and mix well.

3. Wash and cut vegetables. Arrange ingredients attractively on a large plate or platter, placing bowl of marinade meat and vegetables around outside, and bowl of unbroken eggs in center. Meat should be mixed into marinade a few minutes before using.

54

4. Heat at the table either an electric skillet or a heavy iron frypan on a *hibachi*.

5. If using an electric frypan, heat to 420°, add oil and ⅓ of the meat, and stir a few seconds. Reduce heat to 375° and add a portion of each of the vegetables and enough bouillon to moisten. Add part of the marinade and cook until meat and vegetables are tender, 3 to 5 minutes.

6. Then break egg into center of the pan, stir gently into mixture. If desired, sprinkle pine nuts over and serve in individual bowls immediately.

7. Repeat above process until all food is used. Serves 4-5 persons.

❦ KOOK SOO (NOODLES)

Kook soo is a very popular dish because it represents "long life." Although it is served like soup it can also be served as a dish in itself with KIM CHEE *for breakfast (hot), lunch (cold), and as a late evening snack (hot or cold). In Korea* KOOK SOO JIP *(noodle restaurants) are the most prevalent, because noodles are easy to cook, light, and inexpensive. When Koreans meet friends in the street they often say, "Let's have* KOOK SOO," *just as you would say, "Let's have a cup of coffee," in the United States. If you visit a Korean church or friends, you have an opportunity to see how much Koreans like* KOOK SOO *and* KIM CHEE. *If you can eat* KOOK SOO *with your chopsticks then you can say you are mastering the art of using chopsticks. My three American-born children like* KOOK SOO, *hot or cold. I always keep at least one box of dried noodles (which you can buy from any Chinese or Japanese grocery store) because my husband insists on*

KOOK SOO *at least once a week. If you want to serve cold noodles wait until the hot soup becomes cold, then add a few pieces of ice cubes in the soup.*

1 pound package Oriental noodles, fresh or dried	2 tablespoons soy sauce
1/4 pound meat (beef, pork or chicken)	1 tablespoon toasted sesame seeds
2 green onions, chopped	1 teaspoon salad oil
1 clove garlic, minced	Salt and pepper to taste
	1/2 teaspoon monosodium glutamate
	Egg garnish (*see page 35*)

1. If using dried noodles, add noodles, 1 teaspoon salt, 2 to 3 drops oil to prevent sticking to several quarts of boiling water, stirring enough to keep them from sticking together. Then add one cup of cold water. Bring to boil again and boil for 5 minutes. Rinse in cold water. If using fresh noodles, proceed as for dried noodles except after bringing to boil the second time, remove from heat immediately and rinse.

2. Chop meat into about 1/2 inch cubes. Chop green onions, reserving a small handful of the tops for a garnish. Mince garlic.

3. Preheat sauce pan, put in all above ingredients except noodles and garnish. Sauté until meat is well cooked. Add hot water and simmer about 20 to 30 minutes.

4. Put drained noodles in individual bowls and cover with the boiling hot soup.

5. Decorate the top with egg and onion garnishes. Serves 5-6 persons.

NOTE: This makes a good lunch soup. In Korea it is also used for a late evening snack.

❦ CHOP CHAI (COMBINATION DISH WITH MEAT, VEGETABLES AND NOODLES)

CHOP CHAI *means a combination of vegetables, but it also contains a variety of meat, (beef, pork, or chicken, depending on one's choice) noodles, (bean noodles or* FUN SHEE *in Chinese are best) and mushrooms.* CHOP CHAI *is an ideal buffet dish for a large crowd. An artistic arrangement of* CHOP CHAI *on the dinner table reflects the personality of the host, and the beauty of the dish appeals to the eyes of the guests. This dish is served hot in winter, cold in summer.*

¼ pound bean noodles (*fun shee*)
　or if unavailable substitute
　vermicelli
½ pound beef tenderloin
1 clove garlic, minced
½ bunch green onions
2 tablespoons soy sauce
1 tablespoon toasted crushed
　sesame seeds
　Dash of pepper
½ pound fresh bean sprouts

1 or 2 carrots
½ can bamboo shoots
3 to 5 mushrooms (Oriental
　mushrooms)
2 medium dry onions
　Salad oil for frying
1 tablespoon sugar
1 teaspoon monosodium glutamate
1 teaspoon salt
　Egg garnish (*see page 35*)

1. Bring a quart or more of water to boil. Add noodles and boil 3 to 5 minutes. Stir once while cooking. Rinse in cold water and drain well. Turn out on cutting board and cut across several times. This will result in pieces about 6 inches long.

2. Slice tenderloin thinly, slice in another direction to make thin strips. Cut across these strips. This will resemble coarsely ground beef. Or I recommend asking the butcher for coarsely ground lean beef. The taste

difference will be slight. Add minced garlic, one chopped green onion, half of the soy sauce, sesame seeds and pepper, saving the remainder for later use. Then mix well and fry in a small amount of oil until meat is tender. Remove from pan and set aside.

3. Add fresh bean sprouts to boiling water and boil for 3 minutes. Drain well.

4. Slice carrots, diagonally, very thin. Lay slices flat and cut into slivers. Again you may cut preparation time by shredding carrots. Cut bamboo shoots in half and slice each half diagonally. Slice mushrooms into thirds. Slice dry onions lengthwise thinly.

5. Put one tablespoon of oil in a skillet and when hot add carrot strips. Fry slowly until tender, stirring constantly, about 3 minutes. Remove carrots and set aside. Add a little more oil to pan and fry bamboo shoots and mushrooms together in the same manner. Remove and repeat with dry onion.

6. In a large bowl combine all ingredients, noodles, meat, and vegetables. Season with sugar, monosodium glutamate, and remainder of sesame seeds, soy sauce and pepper. Salt to taste. Mix lightly, turn into a frypan and heat through about 5 minutes. Garnish with egg and remainder of chopped green onions.

In Korea this would be served cold in the summertime. Serves 8 persons.

❦ KIM CHEE (KOREAN PICKLES)

KIM CHEE *is the famous pickle of Korea, served at almost any meal the year around. It is made from Korean cabbage (in this country Chinese cabbage can be used) with a mixture of seasonings. In Korea, November is the* KIM CHEE *season, because most families prepare the whole year's supply of* KIM CHEE *at this time. It has a strong odor but you will learn to like it. The late Dr. George McCune, one of the outstanding American missionaries and president of Sung-sill College in Pyongyang for many years, was a great devotee of* KIM CHEE. *When he returned to the United States in 1941, because of Japanese pressure against American missionaries, he was seasick and lost his appetite. After he landed in Los Angeles, one of the largest Korean communities in America, the first thing he asked from his Korean friends was, "Do you have* KIM CHEE *for me?"*

Koreans cannot think of any true Korean dinner without KIM CHEE *and rice. Korean students and tourists abroad seem to miss* KIM CHEE *more than any other food. Recently, I had the opportunity of trying* KIM CHEE *on my American friends who had never had it before, when I prepared a Korean dinner for the San Francisco YWCA. I filled a one-gallon jar with* KIM CHEE *without using too much garlic and hot pepper. Believe it or not, the forty guests, including some Chinese who also tasted Korean food for the first time, cleaned up the whole jar of* KIM CHEE. *The following recipe is for American friends, from Chinese cabbage.*

5 to 6 pounds Chinese cabbage	1 teaspoon sugar
4 or more tablespoons salt	1½ tablespoons paprika
2 cloves garlic, minced	2 teaspoons salt
3 or 4 green onions, finely chopped	2 teaspoons monosodium glutamate
2 teaspoons fresh ginger root, minced, or 1 teaspoon ginger powder	½ to 1 teaspoon cayenne pepper or red chile pepper
	2 or more cups water

1. Separate cabbage leaves, wash, and cut into 1½-inch lengths.

2. Sprinkle 4 tablespoons salt evenly over cut cabbage and let stand at least 2 or 3 hours.

3. Add garlic, onions, ginger, sugar, paprika, salt, monosodium glutamate and red pepper to the cabbage. Mix thoroughly. Pack tightly in a glass quart jar to 2 inches of the top.

4. Pour in enough water to cover. Keep tightly covered with lid.

5. Let stand for several days at room temperature to ripen before serving. Serves 10-12 persons.

NOTE: In warm weather the pickle may be eaten within 24 hours. *Kim Chee* can be kept for several weeks in the refrigerator after ripening. In some areas *Kim Chee* may be purchased in food stores.

RICE

RICE *has been and still is one of the three basic foods (*SOUP *and* KIM CHEE *are the other two) of the Korean people. They eat rice three times a day, just as bread is served with each meal in America. Rice production is usually still done by human labor, for planting, reaping, and threshing; the water buffalo is used only for the cultivation of land. My husband, who was raised in a small farm village, often told me how much he loved to live in the country. When you travel the countryside in the spring you can hear the farmers singing as they plant rice seeds; in the summer as the rice plants grow the fields are covered with the green leaves of the rice blades; in the autumn the fields gradually turn into waves of yellow as the wind ripples them. The rice harvest time is the happiest season for the farmers. As the people eat rice they often think of the Chinese proverb: "Each single grain contains a farmer's hard labor."*

There are many kinds of rice dishes, but BIBIM BAHB *(rice mixed with vegetables and meats) is the typical Korean rice dish. According to the Korean tradition, the dish is used as a midnight snack on December 31 every year. It is a "good-bye dish" to the old year, and usually the left-over white rice of the day is used as its basic materials. Today some of the Korean restaurants specialize in* BIBIM BAHB. *Korean families often serve it for lunch or a late-evening snack.*

❧ BASIC RICE PREPARATION

The method of rice-cooking is the same in China, Japan, and Korea. All that differs is the kind of rice used. Chinese use a long grain rice, commonly called Texas rice in this country. The Japanese and Koreans use either patina or Blue Rose, now commonly called California rice. These are short and round grained rices. Blue Rose is considered to have better flavor and is more expensive.

HOW TO COOK RICE:

1. Wash rice with cold water several times, running cold water into pan, stir briefly, then drain.

2. For one cup of uncooked rice, use 1½ to 2 cups of cold water. The Oriental cook does not measure the water, but sticks her thumb on top of the rice and pours water in until it reaches the first knuckle (about one inch). Use a heavy, deep pan with a tight-fitting cover.

3. Soak the rice at least 1 to 2 hours. This is most important because it makes the rice fluffy.

4. Bring to boil over high heat.

5. When it starts to boil, lower the heat and slowly simmer about 8 to 10 minutes, covered.

6. Turn the heat high once more. Watch carefully at this point and turn heat off after all extra moisture has escaped as steam. This will take about 2 minutes.

7. Turn off heat and keep covered for another 5 to 7 minutes. If covered too long, rice will become sticky; therefore, take cover off and mix lightly so that the rice will loosen from the pan.

❧ RICE WITH RED BEANS (PAHT BAHB)

½ cup dried red beans (these can be purchased in a Japanese grocery or you may use any type of red beans)

3 to 4 cups water
2 cups rice

1. Wash the beans well, then add 3 or 4 cups water to beans in pot. Cover and bring to a boil. Reduce heat and simmer about 25 to 30 minutes or more until beans are tender.

2. Wash rice and drain well. For directions on how to prepare rice, *see page 62*. Add cooked beans and bean water to rice. Cover pot tightly and bring to a boil quickly. Reduce heat and simmer about 20 to 25 minutes. Turn off heat and leave on stove another seven minutes. Do not stir or remove cover during this time.

3. After the seven minutes, remove lid and stir rice, otherwise it will be sticky. Serves 5-6 persons.

NOTE: This makes a very pretty as well as delicious variation of rice. You might also wish to try sweet potatoes with rice—just peel and cut potatoes into ½-inch cubes, put raw into uncooked rice, and cook as above, only a few minutes longer.

❧ RICE WITH MUSHROOMS (SONGI BAHB)

2 cups rice
¼ pound lean beef, chopped or ground

½ pound fresh mushrooms, sliced
1 onion, sliced
2 tablespoon soy sauce

63

Dash of pepper
1 tablespoon salad oil
2 teaspoons toasted, crushed
sesame seeds

¼ teaspoon monosodium glutamate
Handful cooked peas
Egg garnish (*see page 35*)

1. Wash rice carefully and soak in water at least an hour. (Grains separate easily and are fluffy.)

2. Mix together chopped or ground beef, mushrooms, onions, soy sauce, pepper, oil, toasted sesame seeds and monosodium glutamate. Cook a few minutes.

3. Add slightly cooked meat mixture to the rice and add water and salt, cover tightly and bring to a boil.

4. Reduce heat and simmer 25 to 30 minutes. (Do not stir or remove the lid while cooking.)

5. Place egg garnish and few cooked peas in bottom of a large round rice bowl. Add cooked rice mixture and gently press down. Then turn upside down on serving plate. The garnish will then be on top. Serves 5-6 persons.

❦ RICE MIXED WITH VEGETABLES AND MEAT (BIBIM BAHB)

1½ cups rice
½ pound lean ground beef or top
round cut in thin strips
4 tablespoons soy sauce
1 tablespoon salad oil

2 green onions
2 cloves garlic
2 tablespoons toasted,
crushed sesame seeds
Dash of pepper

1 teaspoon sugar
½ teaspoon monosodium
    glutamate
1 to 2 cups bean sprouts
2 tablespoons oil for frying
1 cup celery, thinly sliced

1 cup cucumber, thinly sliced
2 carrots
1 4-ounce can water chestnuts,
    sliced thin
Salt to taste

GARNISH:

1 green onion, slivered
Egg garnish (*see page* 35)

Sprinkle of toasted sesame seeds
Toasted almonds (optional)

1. Cook rice following recipe on *page 62*. This will yield 3 to 4 cups cooked rice.

2. Mix together well the ground beef, soy sauce, salad oil, green onions, garlic, sesame seeds, pepper, sugar and monosodium glutamate. Cook slowly in frying pan until meat is done, stirring frequently.

3. Add whole bean sprouts and cook until they are heated through (do not overcook). Remove from heat. If canned bean sprouts are used, drain well before using.

4. Cut celery very thin on the diagonal, sprinkle with salt lightly and let stand for 15 minutes. With your hands, squeeze the water from the celery. Peel cucumber only if skin is tough; slice diagonally very thin. Peel carrots, cut into 1-inch lengths and with sharp knife shred each piece lengthwise. (You may use a shredder if time is limited.) Cook carrots in salted boiling water for about three minutes.

5. In a second frying pan, put two teaspoons oil and fry celery for about two minutes. Remove and add to meat mixture. Add two more teaspoons

oil and fry the cucumber for two minutes. Remove and add to meat mixture. Drain carrots and fry in oil then add these to meat mixture.

6. Slice the water chestnuts thin, and add them to the meat and vegetable mixture and then mix gently with hot cooked rice. Salt to taste.

7. May be served in bowls or on plates. Decorate each serving with egg garnish, slivered green onions, and sesame seeds or toasted almond. Serves 5-6 persons.

DESSERTS

FRESH FRUITS *are commonly served as dessert. Korean apples and pears are very juicy and sweet. Usually the host peels the skins of the apples or pears at the dinner table with a small knife, cuts them into four pieces, and takes the seeds out. Then he sticks tooth picks in each piece and places the dish in the center of the table so that the guests can reach it easily. Besides the fresh fruits, there are many other delicious desserts such as* YAK SHIK, SOOJUNG KWA, *and fruit punches. Some of them will take time for preparation, but you will find the results well worth the effort.*

❧ DRIED PERSIMMONS (SOOJUNG KWA)

1 pound dried persimmons or figs	1 cup brown sugar, firmly packed
4 or 5 slices ginger root	4 cups water

GARNISH:

Cinnamon   Pine nuts

1. Combine ginger and water in sauce pan, bring to boil, and boil about 10 to 15 minutes.

2. Strain out and throw away the ginger pieces. Add brown sugar and bring to boil until sugar is dissolved.

3. Put the persimmons into a bowl and cover with lukewarm ginger and sugar water. Leave at least 5 to 6 hours.

4. To serve, place persimmons into individual dishes and add enough

sugar water to cover. Sprinkle with cinnamon and top with 5 or 6 pine nuts in each dish. Serves 5-6 persons.

❧ CHESTNUT BALLS (YOUL RAAN)

1 pound chestnuts	2 teaspoons cinnamon
3 tablespoons honey, or more	5 tablespoons pine nuts or
1 tablespoon sugar	½ cup walnuts

1. Boil or steam the chestnuts in the shells for 15 to 20 minutes. Remove the shells, skin, and mash well with a potato masher.

2. Add honey, sugar, and cinnamon to the mashed chestnuts.

3. If the mixture is too dry, add 1 teaspoon milk and 2 tablespoons soft butter.

4. Make into balls a little smaller than walnut size.

5. Chop finely the pine nuts or walnuts and roll the small balls in the chopped nuts. Serves 5-6 persons.

❧ DATE BALLS OR DATE SQUARES (CHO RAAN)

1 pound seeded dates	1 teaspoon cinnamon
3 tablespoons sugar	3 tablespoons pine nuts or walnuts

1. If using Korean dates, seed them and steam them for about 15 minutes. This is not necessary if using American dates, as they are less tough.

2. Chop well.

3. Add sugar and cinnamon and shape in balls the size of a small walnut.

68

Roll in finely chopped pine nuts or walnuts, then flatten with palm of hand and shape into squares or bars. Serves 5-6 persons.

NOTE: Korean dates can be purchased in a Chinese food store. The color is bright red.

❧ STEAMED SWEET RICE AND DRIED FRUITS (YAK SHIK OR YAK BAHB)

2 cups sweet rice (*see page 113*)
½ to 1 cup brown sugar
2 tablespoons sesame seed oil
4 tablespoons honey
1 to 2 tablespoons dark molasses
2 tablespoons soy sauce

½ cup cooked chestnuts
(or canned chestnuts)
½ cup Oriental dates or raisins
2 tablespoons pine nuts for
garnishing
½ teaspoon cinnamon

1. Wash the sweet rice under cold water. Leave enough water in pan to cover the rice and let it soak for at least an hour.

2. Drain sweet rice thoroughly and then steam for 20 minutes. Stir at least once while steaming.

3. Remove sweet rice from steamer to large bowl. While hot, add brown sugar, oil, honey, molasses, and soy sauce. Mix thoroughly.

4. Add chestnuts, dates (or raisins) to sweet rice and transfer to steamer again and steam another 45 minutes.

5. Pour sweet rice in any type square dish and press down. Garnish with pine nuts and sprinkle with cinnamon. Cut in desired size pieces and serve with ginger tea. Serves 5-6 persons.

CHINESE FOOD

CHINESE COOKING *has been developed from generation to generation. One can distinguish three different categories: Peking cooking, Canton cooking, and Nanking-Shanghai cooking. The pages that follow consider every aspect of Chinese cooking: nutritional value, palatability, texture, fragrance, and color. Eating together with the members of the family has been and still is a great pleasure in China. The Chinese people consider cooking one of the arts, and cooks are treated as skilled professionals. In the sixth century, the chief cook in wealthy households held the title of "Grand Maestro of the Culinary Art" (*DAAI SEE FOOH*).*

Most Chinese cooking requires systematic preparation: meat is sliced or chopped, mixed with flavoring ingredients, and allowed to soak from ten to fifteen minutes; vegetables are cleaned and laid aside in neat piles on a dish; dried ingredients are soaked in warm water until spread out, and then cleaned in fresh cold water. Thus all needed materials are well prepared and laid out within easy reach before the actual cooking starts.

Generally, the process of Chinese cooking is as follows: If the ingredients are to be fried, braised or browned, always heat the pan first, *then pour in the oil and heat until it is thin and easy-flowing before the ingredients are added. If oil or water is required during the cooking, it is added by pouring the minimum amount down the side of the pot or pan. Use hot water for the addition, unless the recipe calls for cold water. (Very little water is used in most Chinese cooking, because the method of quick cooking brings out the needed juices from the meat and vegetables.)*

Chinese methods of cooking meat and fish are deep-frying, steaming, roasting, stewing, and smoking. Most Chinese food is thoroughly cooked but some of the vegetable dishes are only half-cooked.

There are many Chinese kitchen utensils, such as steam lanterns, cleavers, chopping blocks, pastry boards, and rollers, but the Chinese wok *(frying pan) made of thin iron or copper is the most useful single utensil, excellent for frying and braising. A* wok *can be purchased in any local Chinese store.*

Basic ingredients of all Chinese cooking are rice, Chinese pea pods, bean sprouts, Chinese scallions, parsley, Chinese cabbage, BOK CHOY, *and dried mushrooms. The principal seasonings are oyster sauce, sesame oil,* HOISIN *sauce, five-spice mixture (anise, cinnamon, star anise, cloves, and fennel), bean cake, mustard, and peanut oil.*

The most popular Chinese foods are fried rice, fried shrimps, sweet and sour spareribs, almond or roast duck, roast chicken, CHOW MEIN, EGG FOO YUNG, *steamed fish, egg-flour soup, and shark's fin soup.* MEIN *or noodles are generally served at birthdays and feast days, and the guests are invited to partake of this dish in large portions, which signifies their desire to wish long life and happiness to the person in whose honor the party is given.*

72

SOUP

THE CHINESE *use various materials for soup stock—pork, beef, chicken, or ham, and rarely throw away meat bones because they can be used for slow-cooking soups. A soup gets its taste from what is in it. There are two kinds of soups, light and heavy. A light soup is generally served as a drink between courses. Its ingredients are used for flavoring and it usually follows a fried dish like deep-fried shrimps. Heavy soup is often a meal in itself. At formal dinners it is a main dish and served at the end of the meal.*

When a Chinese friend says to you, "Drop in this evening, I have some soup," you can be sure that you will have a heavy soup, with a whole chicken in it, or a whole shad. In China soup is served several times at a big dinner. At an ordinary meal, there is usually a big bowl of soup on the table from which you help yourself with your spoon. In this country the Chinese restaurants serve soup at the beginning of the meal and remove the empty soup bowl usually before you start on other dishes.

❧ ABALONE SOUP (BOW YU TONG)

¼ pound lean pork	2 thin slices fresh ginger
1 teaspoon soy sauce	6 cups boiling water
½ teaspoon sugar	2 teaspoons salt
1 teaspoon cornstarch	2 or 3 dried mushrooms (Oriental)
1 tablespoon oil (vegetable or sesame)	2 or 3 stalks celery
	½ can abalone—12-ounce size
½ teaspoon black pepper	1 green onion, chopped for garnish

1. Slice pork into very thin strips and mix with soy sauce, sugar cornstarch, ½ tablespoon of oil and pepper.

2. Heat remainder of oil in a pan, fry ginger with salt for a minute, and then add 6 cups boiling water.

3. Soak mushrooms 15 minutes in warm water, then slice mushrooms and celery.

4. Cut abalone into thin strips or thin cubes.

5. When water reboils, add mushrooms, celery, and seasoned pork.

6. Cover pot with lid and simmer about 8-10 minutes.

7. Just 5 minutes before serving, add abalone. Do not overcook abalone, because it will become tough.

8. Add green onion and serve immediately. Serves 5-6 persons.

NOTE: You should have no problem using up the other half can of abalone. It is already seasoned in the can, so is delicious served thinly sliced over a bed of lettuce. You might wish to have a soy sauce dip on the side for added flavor.

❧ CHICKEN AND VEGETABLE SOUP

A very good company soup.

1 chicken breast, sliced very thin
¼ teaspoon salt
    Dash of pepper
1 teaspoon monosodium glutamate
2 teaspoons cornstarch

½ can of bamboo shoots, sliced thin
1 dried mushroom, sliced thin, or
    large fresh mushroom, sliced thin
5 or 6 sugar peas (optional)

SOUP BASE:

4 cups chicken soup stock, or
    chicken bouillon
    Salt to taste
    Dash of pepper
1 teaspoon monosodium glutamate

2 teaspoons soy sauce
½ teaspoon sesame oil (or other
    cooking oil)
    Green onion, finely chopped
    crosswise

1. Slice chicken meat in thin slices and sprinkle with salt, pepper and monosodium glutamate. Mix 2 teaspoons cornstarch with 2 tablespoons water and dip meat into mixture. Then put into boiling water for about 2 minutes; drain well.

2. Put fresh vegetables into lightly salted water and bring to boil and cook only 2 minutes. Drain well.

3. Divide meat and vegetables into individual soup bowls.

4. Boil soup stock with salt, pepper, monosodium glutamate. Salt lightly as soy sauce will increase salty flavor. Turn off heat, then add soy sauce and oil.

5. Pour over meat and vegetables in soup bowls; sprinkle with green onions and serve hot. Serves 5-6 persons.

❦ PORK MEATBALL SOUP

MEATBALLS:

½ pound ground lean pork
½ teaspoon salt
1 tablespoon cornstarch
Dash pepper

1 green onion, finely chopped
1 egg
1 teaspoon ginger root, grated or
⅛ teaspoon powdered ginger

SOUP BASE:

4 cups soup stock of any kind, or
canned bouillon
3 dried mushrooms, finely chopped
1 green onion, chopped

1 tablespoon soy sauce
Dash of salt and pepper
1 egg

1. To ground pork, add salt, cornstarch, pepper, chopped green onion, egg, ginger and mix thoroughly. Roll into small walnut-size meatballs.

2. Bring soup stock to boil, put in meatballs and cook until done (5 to 7 minutes).

3. Then add mushrooms, green onion, soy sauce, salt and pepper; lightly beat 1 egg and gently drop into soup while stirring. Cover and cook one minute. Pour into soup bowls. Serves 5-6 persons.

NOTE: Try chicken, beef, fish soup stocks, or canned consommé. If you use dried Oriental mushrooms, before using soak in water for 30 minutes to 1 hour. Fresh mushrooms may be substituted where Chinese dried mushrooms are unavailable—flavor will be slightly changed.

FISH AND SEA FOOD

CHINESE LIKE *fresh fish. Some of the Chinese fish markets, like the one in Chinatown in San Francisco, have a big fish vat where the live fish swim around. The Chinese keep the fish in vats until they are needed. One of the secrets of cooking fish the Chinese way is to use wine, ginger, or vinegar to avoid the fishy taste. Since it is difficult to get the right kind of fish for Chinese cooking in this country, I have introduced just a few fish dishes, including four shrimp dishes. The proper preparing of shrimp dishes begins with good marketing, that is, be sure to buy fresh shrimps. The fresher shrimps are bluish, and they get pinkish or whitish as they become less fresh. Keep them in the icebox until used.*

❦ STEAMED FISH (JING YU)

1 medium-size flat fish (sea bream or other white fish)
½ teaspoon salt
½ teaspoon sugar
1 tablespoon soy sauce
½ teaspoon monosodium glutamate
Dash of pepper
1 tablespoon sesame seed oil or salad oil

2 dried mushrooms (before using, soak them in warm water and then shred)
2 green onions, diagonally sliced
1 clove of garlic, minced
2 slices of fresh ginger, shredded
2 teaspoons cornstarch

1. Clean the fish thoroughly and wipe off excess water. Place the fish in an attractive heat-proof dish.

2. Combine ¼ teaspoon salt, ¼ teaspoon sugar, ½ tablespoon soy sauce, ½ teaspoon monosodium glutamate, and dash of pepper. Rub into fish and let it stand for about 15 minutes.

3. Slice soft mushrooms and green onions and mix with remaining ingredients, salt, sugar, soy sauce, oil, and cornstarch. Spread this mixture over top of the fish.

4. Place fish in steamer and steam about 20 minutes. Serve while it is hot. Serves 2-3 persons.

❧ FRIED WHOLE FISH WITH SWEET AND SOUR SAUCE

1 whole fish, bass or carp (about 3 pounds or less)
2 tablespoons sherry or cooking wine
1 tablespoon soy sauce
2 tablespoons cornstarch
Oil for deep frying
3 dried mushrooms (before using soak in warm water, then shred)

½ can bamboo shoots (optional)
½ carrot, shredded
1 or 2 green onions, diagonally sliced
1 or 2 teaspoons sliced fresh ginger, shredded
1 clove garlic, minced
1 tablespoon oil

SWEET AND SOUR SAUCE:

4 tablespoons sugar
3 tablespoons vinegar
3 tablespoons soy sauce

1 teaspoon monosodium glutamate
1 cup cold water
1 tablespoon cornstarch

1. Clean fish thoroughly. Score both sides of fish about 3 times.

2. Combine sherry, soy sauce and salt. Rub this mixture on both sides of the fish. Let it stand for about 30 minutes.

3. Just before frying, take the fish out of the marinade and rub both sides with cornstarch. Heat oil and fry the fish about 15 minutes until golden brown. (If fish is large, after frying, bake in a 350° oven for 25 minutes.)

4. Heat oil; sauté mushrooms, bamboo shoots, carrots, green onions, ginger, and garlic; then add sweet and sour sauce ingredients.

5. Mix cornstarch in water; add it to the above ingredients and cook until thick. Stir constantly.

6. Set the fried fish on an attractive large plate and pour the sweet and sour sauce on top; serve immediately. Serves 5-6 persons.

NOTE: Fish may be deep fried in advance before serving. Refry the fish to make it more crispy.

❧ TUNA FISH

1 can (6 ounce) tuna, chunk style	½ cup green pepper, coarsely chopped
1 teaspoon butter or cooking oil	2 teaspoons soy sauce
½ cup blanched almonds, split in half	½ teaspoon monosodium glutamate
1 cup water	2 teaspoons cornstarch
½ teaspoon salt	4 teaspoons cold water
1 medium onion, sliced thin	3 to 4 cups hot cooked rice

1. Place butter and almonds in a shallow pan and lightly brown them in a 300° oven for about 20 minutes or fry over a low heat in frying pan. Shake the pan 2 or 3 times while roasting or frying.

2. Put the water, salt, green pepper and onion in a saucepan. Cover and cook until pepper is tender but still crisp.

3. Stir in almonds, tuna, soy sauce and monosodium glutamate.

4. Mix cornstarch and cold water together and add to tuna mixture; cook until thick, stirring constantly.

5. Serve over hot rice. Serves 5-6 persons.

NOTE: Deep-fried noodles may be substituted for hot rice.

❦ SKEWERED SHRIMP

1 pound large, raw shrimps	3 or 4 strips of bacon cut into
1 5 oz. can water chestnuts, cut in halves	squares

MARINADE:

¼ cup soy sauce	½ teaspoon ginger, grated or
¼ cup dry sherry	⅛ teaspoon powdered ginger
¼ cup peanut oil	1 clove garlic, minced

1. Shell, devein, and split open large shrimp. Soak them in the above sauce for 30 minutes.

2. Thread the shrimp on either metal or bamboo skewers with sliced water chestnuts and squares of bacon.

3. Broil them over hot charcoal or in broiler, turning several times and basting with the marinade.

4. Serve hot with cooked rice. Serves 5-6 persons.

❦ SHRIMPS IN BLACK BEAN AND GARLIC SAUCE (CHOW HAR)

1 pound shrimps	2 tablespoons peanut oil

1 tablespoon black beans, canned
1 clove garlic, chopped fine
¼ teaspoon fresh ginger root, grated
1 tablespoon cornstarch

2 tablespoons tomato catsup
½ teaspoon monosodium glutamate
2 green onions, diagonally sliced or green pepper strips
Pepper and salt to taste

1. Remove black vein of shrimps with a toothpick. Poke toothpick in the back at the center to take out the black vein, leaving shells on.

2. Wash shrimps and black beans.

3. Sauté garlic, grated ginger root, and black beans in heated peanut oil in a large frying pan. Put shrimps in and cook until pink in color.

4. Blend cornstarch, tomato catsup, and monosodium glutamate in ¼ cup water.

5. Add the mixture to the shrimps and cook until thick.

6. Garnish with sliced green onions or pepper strips.

7. Serve hot with hot cooked rice. Good for dieting. Serves 5-6 persons.

NOTE: Buy already seasoned dried black beans at Chinese food store. Can be bought in any quantity.

❦ CHINESE FRIED SHRIMP BALLS

1 pound raw shrimps cleaned; grind or chop fine
1 teaspoon salt
2 tablespoons cornstarch

Dash of pepper
1 egg
Oil for deep frying

1. Mix ground shrimps, salt, cornstarch and dash of pepper. Beat egg separately, add slowly to shrimp mixture, stirring. You may not need all the egg, as mixture should not be too soft.

2. When making shrimp balls, put a little cornstarch on your hands to prevent sticking and roll balls between palms of your hands. Make shrimp balls walnut size and deep fry about 2 or 3 minutes, until golden brown. Put only 5 or 6 shrimp balls into hot oil at one time.

3. Serve with Sweet and Sour Sauce or soy sauce with mustard. (*see page 84.*) Serves 5-6 persons.

❧ BUTTERFLY SHRIMPS (WU DIP HAR)

1 pound large shrimps, fresh or frozen

2 to 4 cups oil for deep frying

BATTER:

1 cup enriched flour, sifted
1 to 2 teaspoons cornstarch
1 egg, slightly beaten
1 cup water

¼ cup milk
Dash of salt and monosodium glutamate

1. Clean and shell the shrimps, but do not remove the tails. Remove the black veins of the shrimps.

2. Make batter by combining the ingredients. The secret for a good batter and tasty shrimps is to combine the ingredients but not to stir too much. It is also important not to get too much batter on shrimps.

3. Dip shrimps into the light batter and fry in hot oil about 3 to 5 minutes at 365° until golden brown. Serves 5-6 persons.

NOTE: The most important factor to remember in deep frying is to put in only 5 or 6 shrimps at a time, because otherwise the temperature will go down and the shrimps will not be crisp.

PORK DISHES

When the *Chinese say "meat," they mean pork unless some other kind of meat is specified. It is the most common meat in China. The Chinese eat everything—even the entrails and the skin. Usually pork is sliced very thin so that it can be easily and quickly cooked; different dishes need different kinds of cuts. Pork is cooked with various other ingredients as indicated in the recipes. Some pork-cooking is time-consuming: barbecuing pork shoulder, for example, takes hours. But most Chinese do not mind this, because it is as important and delicious a dish as roast beef in this country. My barbecued pork recipe (*char shue*) *will not take much time, because only two or three pounds of lean pork are needed. Pork should not be eaten unless well done. The right kind of sauce is very important for the pork dishes so I list the sauce recipes first.*

❦ BASIC BARBECUE SAUCE NO. 1

Mix together:

½ cup soy sauce
1 tablespoon honey
2 tablespoons brown sugar
1 clove garlic, minced
  Dash of pepper

1 teaspoon fresh ginger root
  (grated) or ⅛ teaspoon
  powdered ginger

❧ BASIC BARBECUE SAUCE NO. 2

Mix together:

½ cup soy sauce
2 tablespoons brown sugar
1 tablespoon honey
1 teaspoon ginger root, grated or
⅛ teaspoon powdered ginger
1 clove garlic, minced

1 tablespoon tomato catsup
4 drops of Worcestershire sauce
1 tablespoon sherry
¼ teaspoon monosodium glutamate
Dash of black pepper (fresh ground)

❧ GINGER SAUCE (BARBECUE SAUCE)

½ cup soy sauce
1 clove garlic, crushed or minced
½ teaspoon fresh ginger root, grated
¼ cup sherry

¼ cup tomato catsup
1 teaspoon brown sugar
½ teaspoon monosodium glutamate

Mix together and use as marinade for pork or spareribs or for basting meat.

❧ PLUM SAUCE

1 cup plum jam
1 tablespoon vinegar
1 teaspoon onion, grated

¼ teaspoon ginger, grated
Dash of cayenne

Combine in small saucepan, heat to boiling point. Cook about 5 minutes stirring often—then cool. For use on egg rolls.

NOTE: This can be purchased ready-made in a Chinese grocery.

❧ SWEET AND SOUR SAUCE

1 cup stock or water

2 teaspoons salt

2 tablespoons sugar

1 tablespoon vinegar

1 tablespoon cornstarch

Mix all together and cook until thick, stirring constantly.

❧ RED SAUCE

3 tablespoons catsup

3 tablespoons chili sauce

3 tablespoons horseradish

1 teaspoon lemon juice

Dash of Tabasco sauce

Salt and pepper to taste

Mix well and serve with fried or boiled shrimp as appetizer. Keeps in refrigerator for several days.

❧ CHINESE MUSTARD

2 tablespoons boiling water

2 tablespoons dry English mustard, (Coleman's or any good grade)

$\frac{1}{4}$ teaspoon salt

1 teaspoon salad oil

1. Stir boiling water into dry mustard. Add salt and salad oil. If too hot, add 2 or 3 drops of vinegar. To serve, mix with soy sauce if desired.

2. Serve with shrimp, barbecued meat, chop suey, etc.

❧ CHINESE BARBECUED PORK (CHAR SHUE)

2 to 3 pounds lean pork roast, preferably loin

$\frac{1}{2}$ teaspoon salt

5 tablespoons soy sauce

1 tablespoon tomato catsup

$1\frac{1}{2}$ tablespoons honey or brown sugar

1 clove garlic, minced

1 teaspoon sherry, brandy or cooking wine

Dash Worcestershire sauce

$\frac{1}{4}$ teaspoon or less powdered ginger or grated fresh ginger root

Dash of red wine (for color)— optional

85

1. Cut pork along the grain into strips ½ to 1 inch thick, about 1 to 1½ inches wide and 3 inches long. Sprinkle lightly with salt on both sides and let stand for an hour.

2. Combine other ingredients and marinate pork in this mixture for at least 2 hours. Turn once or twice while marinating.

3. Pre-heat oven at 450°. Roast the meat at high heat for about 15 minutes; reduce the temperature to moderate (350°) and continue roasting for about 45 minutes. Turn once and baste meat with drippings.

4. Before serving, slice diagonally into fairly thin pieces.

5. Serve cold with Chinese mustard and soy sauce. (*see page 85.*) Serves 5-6 persons.

NOTE: This is a typical Chinese hors d'oeuvre. Also, it is good as a garnish for American-Chinese *chow mein* and Chinese fried rice. It can also be used as a main dish, sliced.

❧ SWEET-SOUR SPARERIBS (TIM-SUEN-PI GWAT)

1 to 2 pounds spareribs cut into
   1 to 1½ inch pieces (ask butcher
   for sweet-sour spareribs size)
   Salt
2 tablespoons brown sugar or less
4 tablespoons vinegar
⅛ teaspoon heung new fun spices
2 tablespoons soy sauce
1 egg

1 clove garlic, minced
   Dash of pepper
4 tablespoons cornstarch
4 tablespoons oil
2 green onions, diagonally sliced
1 dry onion, quartered
½ cup canned pineapple cubes
1 green pepper, thinly sliced
   (optional)

1. Parboil spareribs in hot boiling water for about 10 minutes.

2. Drain well and sprinkle salt lightly on both sides.

3. Combine brown sugar, vinegar, spice, soy sauce, egg, garlic, pepper and cornstarch. Mix with spareribs until they are coated with batter.

4. Heat the 4 tablespoons oil in frypan or *wok* and drop in spareribs; cook until rich golden brown. Cover and cook on low heat until well done, about 15 to 20 minutes. Remove excess fat.

5. Add onions, pineapple cubes and green pepper strips; mix well.

6. Pour remaining sweet-sour and soy sauce batter over the ribs. Cover and cook together about a minute or until thick. Serves 5-6 persons.

NOTE: If you desire to make this ahead of time, use oven to reheat spareribs at about 325° for about 10 to 15 minutes. Then add onion, green pepper strips, pineapple cubes. Bake for 5 minutes.

❧ BARBECUED SPARERIBS (SHUE-PI GWAT)

2 to 3 pounds meaty pork spareribs, whole or desired size pieces

1 teaspoon salt

BARBECUE SAUCE:

½ cup soy sauce
¼ cup tomato catsup
2 scant tablespoons honey
2 to 3 drops Worcestershire sauce
1 clove garlic (crushed or minced)

1 tablespoon sherry or other cooking wine
Dash of pepper
1 teaspoon monosodium glutamate
1 tablespoon ginger root grated (less if desired)

1. Sprinkle salt on both sides of the spareribs lightly. Let stand for at least 20 minutes.

2. Combine other ingredients into sauce, marinate the spareribs in this sauce for at least 2 to 3 hours. (Turn once or twice to assure even marination.)

3. Drain off marinade. (Spareribs can be barbecued whole or in desired size pieces.)

4. Preheat oven to 450° for 5 minutes; then put in the spareribs and leave for 10 minutes; reduce temperature to 350° and cook for about 30 minutes.

5. While cooking, turn spareribs over after one side is browned. After both sides are browned, cover top of meat with aluminum foil to prevent burning.

6. Baste with drippings once or twice while cooking. Serves 5-6 persons.

VARIATION:

1. Cut ribs in serving pieces and treat as above, but marinate no more than 10 to 15 minutes.

2. Preheat *wok* or electric frypan to about 425°, brown spareribs on both sides. Lower heat to 225°, add marinade, cover and simmer 45 minutes to 1 hour, until fork-tender. Turn once or twice while cooking. Add 1 small can of pineapple chunks during last 5 or 10 minutes of cooking. Just before serving, add thin round slices of green pepper or chopped green onion for color and cook just a minute or so.

3. Serve with hot plain rice.

❦ PORK SPECIAL

4 or 5 thick pork chops (1½ inch)
  Dash of salt
  Paprika
  Pepper
  Garlic salt
2 tablespoons tomato catsup

1 tablespoon brown sugar
2 tablespoons soy sauce, or less
1 8 oz. can crushed pineapple
¼ teaspoon monosodium glutamate
1 tablespoon cornstarch

1. Trim away fat edges from the chops so that they won't curl up during frying. Sprinkle lightly with salt, pepper, paprika and garlic salt. Let stand at least 1 to 2 hours.

2. Brown the chops slowly in a heavy skillet or electric frypan.

3. Leave chops in electric skillet or turn into casserole if cooking on stove top.

4. Combine catsup, sugar, soy sauce, crushed pineapple and monosodium glutamate. Pour over the browned pork.

5. Bake at 350° for 40 to 45 minutes in electric skillet or oven until chops are thoroughly cooked and fork-tender.

6. Serve with hot rice and crisp vegetables. Serves 5-6 persons.

BEEF DISHES

The Chinese do not eat much beef, partly because of their belief that cattle works for man in the fields and should therefore not be eaten. But Mohammedan Chinese eat beef, and consider pork unclean.

Stir-frying is the common method of cooking beef in China. The beef dishes usually contain vegetables, like bean sprouts, asparagus, or broccoli. Beef can be eaten rare, but in Chinese dishes it should not be too rare.

❧ FRIED BEEF (CHOW YOKE)

1 pound beef tenderloin
2 tablespoons sherry or other white wine
1 tablespoon soy sauce
1 teaspoon sugar
Dash salt
2 egg whites, slightly beaten
2 tablespoons flour
Oil for deep frying

1. Slice meat into thick 2-inch-long strips. Pound lightly with edge of knife to prevent shrinkage (as for Swiss steak).

2. Combine soy sauce, wine, sugar and salt; marinate meat at least 1 hour.

3. Dip each strip in flour and then in slightly beaten egg whites.

4. Deep fry in hot oil 350° to 375° frying only 5 or 6 pieces at a time to insure crispness.

5. Serve with raw sliced cucumber or radishes that have been sprinkled with salt, sugar, vinegar and chilled at least one hour. Serves 5-6 persons.

❦ BEEF IN OYSTER SAUCE

1 pound top round	1 tablespoon cooking wine
2 tablespoons peanut oil	1 teaspoon sugar
1 or 2 cloves garlic, minced	1 cup water or beef broth
1 teaspoon salt, or less	3 or 4 Oriental mushrooms, sliced*
¼ cup soy sauce	1 small can water chestnuts
2 tablespoons Chinese oyster sauce	2 or 3 green onions, chopped

1. Cut top round into 1-inch cubes. Heat the oil in a frypan or *wok* and brown beef and garlic in it.

2. Add the salt, soy sauce, oyster sauce, wine, sugar and water or broth and mix well.

3. Cover and cook over low heat about 15 to 20 minutes. Add mushrooms, water chestnuts, and chopped green onion and cook another five minutes. Serves 5-6 persons.

*NOTE: Oriental mushrooms have to be soaked in warm water for about 20-30 minutes before using.

❧ BEEF WITH ASPARAGUS (LOO-SON NGOW YOKE)

1 pound flank steak or tenderloin
1 teaspoon cornstarch
1 teaspoon salt
2 teaspoons soy sauce
1½ to 2 pounds asparagus, diagonally sliced
2 medium onions

2 tablespoons peanut oil or salad oil
2 cloves garlic, minced
1 tablespoon soy bean paste or soy bean condiment
1 teaspoon salt
1 teaspoon sugar
½ teaspoon soy sauce

1. Trim off from meat as much fat as possible; cut meat against grain in ¼-inch strips.

2. Put meat in bowl and add cornstarch, salt and soy sauce. Mix and let stand while preparing vegetables.

3. Cut asparagus diagonally about 2 inches long. Stop cutting when white part is reached and throw rest away, then wash very carefully and drain well.

4. Cut onions in half lengthwise and crosswise.

5. When the *wok* or frypan is thoroughly heated, add 2 tablespoons oil. When it is bubbling from the heat, add minced garlic and fry just until brown. Add meat, stirring frequently until brown.

6. Add onion and cook a minute, then make a little hollow in center, add soy-bean paste and asparagus. Sprinkle over with salt, sugar, and soy sauce. Cover and cook about 5 minutes. Raise lid and stir frequently while cooking.

7. Serve with cooked rice. Serves 5-6 persons.

❧ BEEF WITH BROCCOLI

1 bunch young broccoli (1½ to 2 pounds)
½ pound flank steak or other beef steak
1 tablespoon sherry wine
1 clove garlic, minced
1 teaspoon fresh ginger, minced or

⅛ teaspoon powdered ginger
1 or 2 tablespoons soy sauce
3 teaspoons sugar
1 tablespoon peanut oil
1 tablespoon cornstarch
Toasted sesame seeds for garnish or toasted almonds

1. Trim off any thick layer of fat and cut steak in halves, using only half of steak. Slice thin strips across the grain.

2. Combine sherry, garlic, ginger, soy sauce and sugar. Toss steak strips in mixture, mixing well.

3. Pare off outer covering of broccoli stalks with vegetable peeler, then cut in pieces 2 inches long. Wash several times and drain well.

4. Heat a 10-inch heavy skillet; add oil and, when very hot, add meat mixture. Cook rapidly until very brown without stirring; turn and brown other side.

5. Add broccoli to the meat, cover and cook until vegetables are slightly cooked, for about 3 minutes. Do not overcook.

6. Mix cornstarch with ¼ cup of water to pour over broccoli, stirring constantly until slightly thickened.

7. Before serving, sprinkle with browned whole sesame seeds or almonds. Serves 5-6 persons.

NOTE: This is a winter dish, good when broccoli is in season. However, you can substitute frozen broccoli if you are careful not to overcook it.

93

CHICKEN DISHES

CHICKEN, DUCK, *and geese are other common meats in the Chinese kitchen. They are prepared in a multitude of ways. Young roosters are used for fried, almond, and paper-wrapped chicken dishes. One large rooster can be used in different ways: the white meat can be sliced to make a stir-frying dish; dark meat and bones for slow-cooking soup. For chicken soup, the Chinese use fat hens. The hen meat in the soup also can be used to make other dishes, if it is not overcooked.*

Most Chinese farmers raise chickens, which is very convenient for them, because they can use one whenever friends or unexpected guests visit. I have selected four chicken dishes and one duck dish. Young roosters are good for these recipes.

❧ CHICKEN CHOP SUEY (GAI PIN)

1 to 2 pound chicken (small fryer)
2 tablespoons oil
¼ cup water
¼ pound fresh mushrooms, sliced
1 small can water chestnuts, sliced

½ can bamboo shoots, sliced
3 stalks celery, diagonally sliced
¼ pound sugar peas
1 teaspoon salt

SAUCE:

1 tablespoon cornstarch
1/4 cup water
1 teaspoon monosodium glutamate

1 teaspoon soy sauce
1 teaspoon sugar

1. Have butcher chop chicken (with bones) into 1-inch pieces or use chicken breast, boned and cut into strips.

2. Fry chicken in oil over high heat. Cook until brown.

3. Add 1/4 cup water and all other ingredients. Cover and cook over medium heat for 10 minutes.

4. Mix sauce ingredients and add, stirring constantly.

5. Serve over rice or fried noodles. Serves 5-6 persons.

❦ PAPER-WRAPPED CHICKEN (JEE BOW GAI)

1/2 to 1 pound chicken breast fillet, raw

1 dozen squares of wax paper cut 4″ x 4″

SAUCE:

1 tablespoon soy sauce
1 teaspoon sugar
1 tablespoon honey
1 clove garlic, minced
1 slice fresh ginger, minced
1/4 to 1/2 teaspoon salt

1/4 teaspoon pepper
Dash of five fragrance powder
1 teaspoon cornstarch
1 tablespoon brandy or sherry
Oil for frying

1. Slice chicken breast into 1 1/2-inch long, 1/4-inch wide, 1/2-inch thick pieces.

95

2. Mix sauce ingredients and add chicken fillets.

3. Place chicken slices in center of wax paper. Fold up bottom corner; fold over side corners, then roll up toward top and secure with a toothpick.

4. Heat oil to deep fry, about 365°. Fry 5 or 6 pieces at a time for 1 to 2 minutes on each side. When the chicken shows through the wax paper, it should be a beautiful rich golden red. Serves 6 persons.

❧ ALMOND CHICKEN

1½ to 2 cups raw breast of chicken finely sliced, or 2 cups diced cooked chicken

2 or 3 tablespoons oil (peanut oil or salad oil)

1 small onion, sliced

1 to 1½ cup celery, sliced

1 cup water chestnuts, sliced

1 cup bamboo shoots (5 oz. can already sliced)

2 cups chicken broth or bouillon

2 tablespoons soy sauce

2 teaspoons monosodium glutamate

1 teaspoon sugar

2 tablespoons cornstarch

¼ cup water

Salt

½ cup or less toasted slivered almonds (for topping)

1. Preheat a large heavy frying pan; add oil and fry the chicken 2 to 3 minutes. Add onion and celery and cook 5 minutes. Then add water chestnuts, bamboo shoots, chicken broth, soy sauce, and monosodium glutamate; mix thoroughly, cover, and cook about 5 minutes more.

2. Blend sugar, cornstarch and cold water; pour over the chicken and cook over high heat, stirring constantly until mixture thickens.

3. Add salt to taste.

96

4. Garnish with toasted almonds. Serves 6 persons.

NOTE: The secret is to avoid over-cooking. When cornstarch mixture is added, be sure to use high heat and stir quickly. Serve chicken with cooked hot rice.

❦ CHINESE FRIED CHICKEN (JAR JEE GAI)

1 frying chicken, cut into serving pieces

MARINADE:

1 teaspoon sugar
1 to 2 tablespoons soy sauce
1 clove garlic, minced
1 teaspoon grated ginger root, or
    ¼ teaspoon ginger powder

1 tablespoon sherry or cooking
    wine
1 to 2 tablespoons cornstarch
¼ cup peanut oil or salad oil for
    frying

1. Combine sugar, soy sauce, garlic, ginger and sherry.

2. Rub each chicken piece with marinade and marinate for 30 minutes.

3. Roll the pieces in cornstarch and fry in hot oil until golden brown.

4. Cover and cook slowly for about 30 minutes until the chicken is fork tender.

5. Serve with crispy vegetables. Serves 5-6 persons.

❦ GINGER DUCK

1 young duck, cut into serving
    pieces
¼ cup soy sauce
1 tablespoon fresh ginger, chopped
    or grated

2 cloves garlic, minced
1 can ring pineapple (small can)
½ cup mushrooms, sliced
4 tablespoons oil (for sauté)

97

1. Combine soy sauce, chopped ginger, and garlic to marinate duck, turning duck several times to coat evenly. Marinate several hours.

2. Sauté the duck in 2 tablespoons salad oil or peanut oil until the pieces are brown on both sides.

3. Slice mushrooms and sauté in salad oil in another frypan until golden brown.

4. Transfer the sautéed duck to an oven-proof casserole dish; add the juice from the can of pineapple. Add the mushrooms and all the sauce left over from marinating and sautéing the duck.

5. Cover and bake in a moderate oven (350°) about 45 minutes to an hour, or until the duck is fork-tender.

6. Sauté pineapple in oil until lightly browned on both sides and serve with the duck. Serves 5-6 persons.

EGG DISHES

EGGS *occupy as important a place in Chinese cooking as in American. They can be used either as the principal ingredient in a dish or with other ingredients as a combination dish. According to Chinese tradition, the egg is the embodiment of the symbol of* YUM *and* YEUNG, *the negative and positive principles of universal life. The yolk* (YEUNG) *represents the sun or the male principle; the white* (YUM), *the earth or the female. Like milk, the egg contains all elements necessary for the development of life, and is as easily digested. I give here the three most popular egg dishes, including* EGG FOO YUNG *(deluxe) to serve when you have company.*

❧ EGG ROLL (CHUEN GUEN)

FILLING:

½ or 1 cup cooked shrimps, diced fine

½ or 1 cup lean pork cooked, diced fine

1 onion, chopped fine

½ cup cabbage, shredded

½ cup celery, minced

1 can water chestnuts, diced fine

2 stalks green onion, chopped fine

99

½ teaspoon salt

1 tablespoon soy sauce

Dash of pepper

1 teaspoon monosodium glutamate

2 teaspoons toasted sesame seeds

2 teaspoons peanut or salad oil

1. Mix together all ingredients for the filling and add seasoning.

2. Slightly fry in oil for about 2 minutes, stirring constantly.

3. Chill mixture.

HOW TO MAKE EGG SKIN FOR ROLLING:

2 eggs

1 cup flour

Pinch of sugar

½ cup water

1 teaspoon salt

Oil for deep frying

1. Beat eggs and add water, flour, salt and sugar. Mix and make a thin, smooth batter.

2. Lightly grease and heat a 6-inch skillet. Measure 3 tablespoons batter into the skillet; tip the skillet to spread the batter thinly over the surface of the skillet. Cook over medium heat until the batter shrinks from the sides of the skillet. Turn over and cook the other side for 1 minute. Remove from pan and set aside to cool on a damp paper towel. Proceed with rest of batter as above; cool on paper towels, stacking egg skins on top of each other.

HOW TO DEEP-FRY EGG ROLLS:

Place 2 tablespoons filling in center of each cooled egg skin; fold two sides over the filling and roll up the egg roll. Seal with paste made from 1 tablespoon flour and 1 tablespoon water plus wooden toothpicks. Deep-fry rolls until golden brown in 365° to 400° hot oil. Serve with mustard, soy sauce or plum sauce. Serves 5-6 persons.

NOTE: Egg rolls may be steamed in hot steaming pot for 15 to 20 minutes instead of deep frying, for lower calories.

❦ EGG FOO YUNG NO. 1

This is a basic recipe.

3 or 4 eggs
¼ cup flour (if using 4 eggs, omit flour)
½ cup diced cooked pork or ham, chicken, shrimp, or crab
½ small chopped onion

½ pound cooked bean sprouts
2 or 3 green onions, chopped
Dash of pepper
½ teaspoon monosodium glutamate
Oil for frying

1. Beat the eggs and mix with the other ingredients.

2. Immediately fry the mixture in a well-greased hot skillet until golden brown on both sides (make the size of thick pancakes).

3. Serve with hot gravy. Serves 5-6 persons.

GRAVY OR SAUCE:

1 cup chicken stock or water
¼ teaspoon salt
1 teaspoon sugar
2 teaspoons monosodium glutamate

1 or 2 teaspoons soy sauce (or more)
1 tablespoon cornstarch

1. If stock is not available, use water and double or triple the amount of monosodium glutamate.

2. Combine all ingredients and cook until thick, stirring constantly (a minute or two); pour over the *Egg Foo Yung* and serve immediately.

❦ EGG FOO YUNG NO. 2 (DELUXE)

Good for company.

4 eggs
½ cup cooked tiny shrimps
  or crab meat
½ pound cooked bean sprouts,
  or 1 can
2 stalks green onions, chopped
1 tablespoon finely chopped
  water chestnuts

1 tablespoon chopped bamboo
  shoots (optional)
3 or 4 mushrooms, chopped
1 teaspoon monosodium glutamate
  Salt and black pepper to taste
2 tablespoons cooking or salad oil
  for frying

1. If canned bean sprouts are used, drain well.

2. Combine all ingredients except salt, monosodium glutamate, and eggs; mix well.

3. Add eggs to the other ingredients. Mix lightly to break the yolks and blend with the whites.

4. Put in a dash of salt and monosodium glutamate last, because this will help prevent the mixture from becoming watery.

5. Drop into a hot skillet and make into a thick pancake size. Cook both sides until golden brown.

6. Serve hot with gravy. (*see page 101 for gravy or sauce.*) Serves 5-6 persons.

VEGETABLES AND SALADS

CHINA *has many vegetables—some of which are never seen in America. Some common vegetables are sweet peas, bamboo shoots, pea-pods, horse beans, pea-vines, radishes, and cabbage. Many grow in spring and summer, but some, like broccoli and green cabbage, grow in the late autumn and winter in the Changchow and Soochow area. One Chinese writer has said: "Whenever needed for use or for trade, the vegetable gardener lifts up the straw cover, perhaps together with a little snow on top, and digs up the plants or the bamboo shoots as needed."*

In most cases, the cooking time for vegetables is extremely short; the original vegetable color is retained and the vegetable remains crisp. Sometimes you cannot distinguish whether the meat is cooked with the vegetables, or the vegetables with the meat. The vegetable dishes contain meat, usually pork, beef, or chicken, and they are cooked just before serving. I limited the recipes to ingredients easily found in this country.

❧ VEGETABLE AND MEAT COMBINATION (BOK CHOY GNOW)

In America, this dish is called Chop Suey.

½ to 1 pound beef tenderloin cut into thin strips
2 tablespoons oil
1 large onion, sliced
1 clove garlic, crushed or chopped fine

Medium *bok choy* (Chinese greens) or celery, sliced diagonally
¼ pound mushrooms, sliced, or 1 small can mushrooms
¼ cup water

SAUCE:

1 teaspoon soy sauce
1 teaspoon cornstarch
1 teaspoon salt

½ teaspoon sugar
¼ cup water
½ teaspoon monosodium glutamate

1. Fry beef in oil over high heat for 3 minutes, stirring constantly.

2. Remove beef from pan.

3. Fry onions and garlic then all other vegetables and add ¼ cup water. Cover and cook for 5 to 8 minutes.

4. Add cooked beef and mix thoroughly with the vegetables.

5. Before serving, add the sauce and cook, stirring constantly until thickened.

6. Serve immediately with cooked hot rice. Serves 5-6 persons.

NOTE: Any vegetable, such as green beans, green pepper or bean sprouts, may be substituted or added. Canned bean sprouts are added at the last when cooking above vegetables.

CHICKEN OR SEA FOOD AND VEGETABLE SALAD

1 package gelatin strips
1 carrot
2 cucumbers

¼ pound chicken, shrimp or
crab meat

DRESSING SAUCE:

2 tablespoons soy sauce
1 teaspoon sugar
3 tablespoons vinegar
½ tablespoon dry mustard

½ teaspoon monosodium glutamate
Chinese parsley or green onion
shredded for garnishing

1. Cut gelatin into 2-inch strips. Soak in cold water for 5 minutes, pour out the water and place strips in a bowl.

2. Pare cucumbers and carrots, cut them into strips, mix them with the gelatin strips and chicken, shrimps, or crab meat.

3. Mix dressing ingredients; pour over the salad and garnish with parsley or green onion, then toss. Serves 5-6 persons.

NOTE: Pour the salad dressing just before serving.

CHINESE SUGAR PEAS WITH WATER CHESTNUTS

¼ to ½ pound raw pork,
finely chopped
1 tablespoon peanut or salad oil
¼ pound Chinese green peas
(sugar peas)

1 can (5 oz.) water chestnuts,
sliced
¼ pound fresh mushrooms
½ cup chicken stock or 1 cube
bouillon dissolved in hot water

GRAVY:

  ¼ cup water
  1 tablespoon cornstarch
  1 tablespoon soy sauce

  1 teaspoon sugar
  1 teaspoon monosodium glutamate

1. Preheat skillet or *wok* and fry meat in hot oil until brown.

2. Add peas, water chestnuts, mushrooms, and stock; cover and cook not more than 3 minutes over high heat.

3. Combine gravy ingredients in a bowl; push vegetables and meat to one side of the pan and cook the cornstarch mixture until thick and then mix gently with the vegetables.

4. Add salt to taste and serve immediately with cooked hot rice. Serves 5-6 persons.

❦ CELERY WITH MUSTARD DRESSING

  3 stalks celery (white part only)
  1 egg for garnish
  (*see page* 35)

  3 slices cooked ham (cut in
    thin strips)
  1 tablespoon toasted sesame seeds
    (*see page* 43)

DRESSING:

  1 to 2 tablespoons vinegar
  2 teaspoons soy sauce
  1 teaspoon sugar

  1 teaspoon salad oil
  1 teaspoon prepared mustard
  ¼ teaspoon monosodium glutamate

1. Slice celery into 1-inch pieces lengthwise: soak in water for about 30 minutes, then drain well.

106

2. Slice ham and egg garnish into thin strips.

3. Put seasonings into bowl and mix well. Add celery, ham, and egg to dressing and mix thoroughly. Arrange attractively on salad dish and sprinkle top with browned sesame seeds. Serves 4 persons.

❧ STANDARD DRESSING FOR SALADS

3 tablespoons vinegar	1 teaspoon sesame oil or salad oil
2 tablespoons sugar	½ teaspoon monosodium glutamate
1 tablespoon soy sauce	1 teaspoon prepared mustard
½ teaspoon salt	Dash of pepper

1. Mix well and pour over salad just before serving.

NOODLES

THE CHINESE *have a variety of noodle dishes. The northern Chinese eat more noodles than their fellows in the central and southern provinces. Noodles are considered a birthday-party dish because they symbolize long life. In China noodles are mostly made by hand, and most Chinese, especially the cooks, master the noodle-making art. There are many different kinds of noodles, but in this country you find either dried noodles, usually wheat-flavored and obtainable in Chinese or American markets, or fresh egg noodles, obtainable only in the big Chinatown markets of San Francisco, Los Angeles, or New York.*

The common way of preparing noodles is to boil them and then to pour soup and pieces of meat (pork, chicken, or beef) on top. These are the soup noodles. A bowl of soup noodles is occasionally eaten as the main dish for lunch but usually the Chinese eat noodles as a between-meal refreshment. The Chinese do not eat cold noodles as Koreans and Japanese do. When the boiled noodles are further stir-fried with other things, they become CHOW MEIN, *one of the most popular dishes in America.*

❧ BROTH NOODLES (TONG MEIN)

½ to 1 pound noodles
½ chicken breast, sliced
3 dried mushrooms or fresh
   mushrooms
½ bunch spinach
1 tablespoon sesame seed oil
   or peanut oil

2 green onions, chopped
   (for garnishing)
1 tablespoon soy sauce (or more)
½ teaspoon sugar
½ teaspoon salt
⅛ teaspoon black pepper
1 teaspoon monosodium glutamate
6 to 8 cups chicken broth

1. Put the noodles in rapidly boiling water, stirring several times to keep them from sticking together and cook 7 to 10 minutes. If using fresh noodles cook only 2 to 3 minutes. Wash in cold water and drain well.

2. Slice chicken.

3. Slice mushrooms (before using, soak dry mushrooms in warm water).

4. Wash and cut spinach into 1½-inch lengths.

5. Heat a little oil in a pan and fry chicken about 2 minutes. Add mushrooms and spinach to the chicken and cook another few minutes.

6. Place the cooked noodles in serving bowl. Arrange chicken, mushrooms, spinach, and chopped onion on top of the noodles.

7. Season broth with soy, salt, sugar, pepper and monosodium glutamate, then pour over the noodles and serve while hot. Serves 4 persons.

HOW TO DEEP FRY FRESH NOODLES:

1. Use any type of frypan or *wok*. Pour oil into pan and heat until oil is very hot—365° to 400°.

2. The secret is to fry a small amount of noodles at a time, separating them quickly with a long fork or chopsticks, and cooking until noodles turn to a very light brown. Turn once, then remove and drain well on absorbent paper.

3. These noodles may be used at once or saved for later. If they are stored, put them into a tight-fitting jar or plastic bag.

4. Whenever you wish to use the stored noodles, put them into a moderate oven at 325° for 7 to 10 minutes before serving.

❧ PORK CHOW MEIN

Typical or authentic Chinese chow mein.

1 pound fresh Chinese noodles
2 tablespoons oil

Dash salt

MEAT-VEGETABLE TOPPING:

1 pound fresh pork tenderloin or shoulder cut into small squares
2 teaspoons oil, peanut or salad
1 teaspoon salt
Dash black pepper
1 clove garlic, minced
1 medium onion, sliced

2 or 3 stalks *bok choy* (Chinese cabbage)
2 or 3 stalks celery
2 dried Chinese mushrooms, sliced (soak in warm water 15 minutes)
½ pound fresh bean sprouts

GRAVY:

¼ cup water or meat broth
1 tablespoon cornstarch
1 teaspoon sugar

2 teaspoons soy sauce (or more)
½ teaspoon monosodium glutamate

110

GARNISH:

¼ cup toasted almonds or *char shue* (thin sliced ham)

1. Boil 2 cups of fresh water, add noodles and dash of salt, return to boil and cook 2 minutes, stirring constantly. Drain well. Add 2 tablespoons oil to heavy frying pan. Put all of drained noodles in hot frypan and fry about 5 minutes each side or until golden brown.

2. Fry diced pork in a heavy hot skillet and season with salt, pepper and garlic. Add sliced onions, *bok choy*, celery, mushrooms and bean sprouts.

3. Cover and cook until vegetables are half tender—about 3 to 5 minutes (depends on the amount of vegetables).

4. Mix ¼ cup water or broth, cornstarch, soy sauce, sugar and monosodium glutamate and pour over meat and vegetables and cook until thickened over high heat.

5. Serve noodles on individual big plates or bowls, cover with meat-vegetable mixture; garnish with toasted almonds or *char shue* (*see page 85*). Serve immediately. Serves 5-6 persons.

NOTE: If fresh Chinese noodles are not available, use dried Chinese noodles and cook double the time shown above. You may substitute chopped green onions or green peppers for garnish.

❧ CHICKEN CHOW MEIN

½ pound fresh Chinese noodles or 1 can deep fried *chow mein* noodles
Oil for deep frying

½ pound cooked meat—shrimp, chicken, or turkey
2 tablespoons oil (peanut or salad)
1 onion, sliced lengthwise

¼ pound mushrooms, sliced
1 small can water chestnuts, diced (optional)
½ can bamboo shoots, drained and diced (optional)
½ pound fresh or canned bean sprouts (1 can)
3 stalks *bok choy*, diagonally sliced

2 or 3 stalks celery, diagonally sliced
3 green onions, chopped
1 teaspoon salt
Dash pepper
¼ cup water
2 tablespoons toasted almonds, *char shue* or ham sliced thin for garnish

GRAVY:

⅛ to ¼ cup water
1 tablespoon cornstarch
1 teaspoon soy sauce

1 teaspoon sugar
1 teaspoon monosodium glutamate
1 tablespoon sherry (optional)

1. Fry noodles according to recipe *page 109.*

2. Heat 2 tablespoons oil in frying pan or *wok.* Put in sliced onion and fry 1 to 2 minutes.

3. Add meat and all other vegetables, except green onions. Add ¼ cup water, cover, and cook about 5 minutes. Do not overcook as vegetables taste better when crisp.

4. Combine gravy ingredients; pour over center of vegetables, stir and cook until thickened.

5. Serve over noodles. Garnish with toasted almonds, or ham. Serve hot. Serves 5-6 persons.

RICE

Since *I explained in the Korean section how to cook rice, I will mention here only that there are two kinds of ordinary rice and one special kind of dessert rice. The latter is a glutinous, short-grained, white opaque rice used either ground or broiled for Chinese desserts. Of the two other kinds, one is long-grained and one oval-grained rice. The long-grained rice is easier to cook and more popular in restaurants and family kitchens; it is also known as Saigon rice and is imported from Thailand. In America it is called Texas rice. The oval-grained rice is harder to cook than the long-grained kind, because during the cooking a sticky coating is formed over the kernels and makes it difficult for additional water to reach them. When the long-grained rice become cold it is good for fried rice.*

❦ FRIED RICE NO. 1

2 cups cooked cold rice
½ pound raw pork or beef, thinly sliced
¼ cup fresh mushrooms, or dried
1 onion, chopped
½ cup cooked peas

1 tablespoon soy sauce
½ teaspoon monosodium glutamate
Salt to taste
1 egg scrambled for garnish
2 green onions, chopped

1. Cook rice (*see page 62*).

2. Cut the meat into small squares and chop the onion fine. If you use dried mushrooms, soak in warm water 30 minutes, then cut into small pieces.

3. Put 2 or 3 tablespoons cooking oil into a frying pan or *wok*. When the pan gets very hot, fry the meat until well browned, then add chopped onion and mushrooms. Stir until onion is heated through but not browned, add rice, and fry slowly until grains are separated.

4. Add seasonings and peas and mix together.

5. Scramble egg in bowl, put in small, hot, dry frying pan, and stir rapidly until it takes on appearance of small kernels.

6. Put scrambled egg and chopped green onions in a rice bowl; pack fried rice firmly in bowl; turn bowl over onto a plate. The egg and onion will be on top for a garnish. Serves 6 persons.

NOTE: Cooked shrimp may be substituted for meat. Add at last minute. Bacon also may be substituted for pork or beef—in this case, substitute catsup for soy sauce.

❧ FRIED RICE (DELUXE) NO. 2

2 to 3 cups cooked rice (cold)
3 tablespoons peanut oil
½ cup cooked and diced chicken, turkey, or barbecued pork
½ cup diced cooked shrimps
½ cup mushrooms, sliced
¼ cup water chestnuts, diced or sliced

Dash salt
¼ teaspoon monosodium glutamate
Pepper to taste
2 eggs
2 to 3 tablespoons soy sauce
2 green onions, finely chopped
½ cup cooked green peas

1. Heat 2 tablespoons oil in a large, heavy frying pan or *wok*; toss in rice gently, stir to take out all the lumps.

2. When rice is hot, add and mix meat, shrimp, mushrooms, and water chestnuts. Save a little meat for garnish.

3. Beat eggs slightly, add salt, monosodium glutamate, and pepper. Make a hole in the center of the rice, pour in the eggs, and cook until semi-cooked.

4. Add soy sauce and green onions and peas; blend thoroughly.

5. Put garnish meat into any sized round bowl. Fill with fried rice and gently press. Turn over onto a plate. The meat will be on the top for garnish. Serves 5-6 persons.

DESSERTS

THERE ARE *many kinds of Chinese desserts such as cakes, cookies, puddings, and fresh fruits. The most popular Chinese dessert in America is fortune cookies, which you can find in any Chinese or Japanese or supermarket. The recipes I list here are simple to make and delicious. Try them, although they will take time to make.*

❦ SWEET POTATO CANDY

Typical Chinese dessert from Nanking and Peking. These must be made at the last minute and may be impractical for some cooks.

1 pound sweet potatoes	1 cup sugar or less
2 cups oil for deep frying	1 teaspoon toasted sesame seeds
1 tablespoon sherry or whiskey	

1. Peel sweet potatoes, cut into pieces. They should be about 2 inches long and ½ to 1 inch thick.

2. Soak sweet potatoes in water for 5 to 10 minutes.

3. After soaking, drain and dry with paper towel.

4. Deep fry the sweet potatoes at 365° until golden brown. Don't fry more than 10 pieces at a time and don't fry too long. Keep warm in oven at 325° until time for serving.

5. Mix 1 tablespoon oil and a cup of sugar; cook until sugar dissolves and begins to crystalize, then add wine and reduce heat, stirring constantly until the mixture gets stringy.

6. Mix with the warm deep-fried potatoes.

7. The serving dish should be greased to prevent the potatoes from sticking to the sides of the dish. Garnish with sesame seeds.

8. When serving, place in front of each guest a bowl of cold water. Use chopsticks to dip the sweet potatoes in cold water and twirl the stringy potato around the chopsticks. Serves 6 persons.

❦ CHINESE SPONGE CAKE (GLUY DAAHN GO)

4 eggs
4 tablespoons sugar
2 tablespoons baking powder

4 tablespoons flour
(or rice powder)

1. Separate eggs; beat egg whites until stiff but not dry.

2. Add egg yolks gradually and gently mix with whites until extremely fluffy and almost stiff enough to hold. This is best done with an egg whip but electric mixer can be used.

3. Sift flour and baking powder together. Fold gently into eggs whites.

4. Line 9-inch layer pan with wax paper or grease pan.

5. Heat large steamer with water; pour batter into the cake pan and place in the steamer.

6. Place a cloth over the top of the pot, right under the lid, to catch the steam drippings; steam about 25 minutes.

117

7. Take cake out of steamer and cool before removing from pan.

8. Serve plain as a light dessert after a rich meal. Serves 5-6 persons.

❧ MANDARIN ORANGE-PUDDING DESSERT (TANJULIN)

1 package vanilla pudding
2 cups milk
1 can (11 oz.) mandarin oranges,
   well drained
½ cup whipping cream

Dash sugar
1 tablespoon sherry (optional)
Toasted almonds, slivered,
   for garnish

1. Prepare vanilla pudding according to directions on the package and cool, or make your own vanilla pudding.

2. Meanwhile whip cream with a little sugar.

3. When pudding cools, mix with whipped cream and chill until set.

4. Before serving, fold in drained mandarin oranges and sherry.

5. Put into individual glass dishes and garnish top with toasted nuts. Serves 5-6 persons.

NOTE: For less calories, use diet pudding and omit whipped cream. Pudding has a tendency to harden on the top while cooling, so sprinkle a little water on the top to prevent hardening.

❧ COCONUT MACAROONS

Simple to make and delicious.

1 can (15 ounce) sweetened
   condensed milk

3 cups shredded coconut
   (8 ounce package)
1 teaspoon vanilla

1. Combine coconut and condensed milk; add vanilla and mix well.

2. Heat oven to 350° about 10 minutes. The oven should be hot before putting the macaroons in to bake.

3. Grease baking sheet very thoroughly and drop the coconut mixture by teaspoonfuls, one inch apart.

4. Bake about 12 to 15 minutes or until golden brown.

5. Remove from baking sheet immediately and cool on rack. Serves 6 persons or more.

NOTE: Serve with ice cream or pudding.

JAPANESE FOOD

JAPANESE FOOD *is simple in preparation and material. It often tastes sweet because much sugar is used in the cooking. The customary artistic arrangement of food on the dinner table reflects the personality of the hosts and the beauty of their country.*

The principal materials required in Japanese cooking are rice, MISO *soup, (soy bean paste), vegetables, and green tea. The most popular dishes are* SUKIYAKI *(beef, vegetable, bean curd and* GONYAKU[1]*),* TEMPURA *(deep-fried fish or vegetables), and* CHAWANMUSHI *(a steamed egg custard preparation).*

The most important flavorings are sugar, MISO, SHOYU *(soy sauce), and vinegar. Red pepper, horse-radish, ground sesame, and peanuts are also used.*

Soy beans are used in Japanese food in various ways: TOFU *(bean curd),* ABURAGE *(fried* TOFU*), bean paste, and* NATTO *(steamed and fermented beans). Seaweeds are also used, such as* NORI *(seasoned laver),* KONBU *(tangle),* WAKAME *(lobe-leafed* UNDARIA*), and others.*

Fish cooking has been particularly developed in Japan. The Japanese

[1]This is yam noodles which may be purchased fresh or canned at any Japanese food store.

eat more fish than meat in comparison with the Chinese and Koreans. The daily fare of the Japanese includes GOHAN *(white rice)*, MISO SHIRU *(*MISO *soup)*, UDON *(wheat-flour noodles)*, SOBA *(buckwheat noodles)*, and fish.

Japanese green tea is one of the national beverages. Before and after meals, the Japanese drink tea. Each member of the family has his own and different cup. Special tea cups, usually of lesser height, and small teapots are set aside for visitors. The tea ceremony, CHANOYU, has been a national custom for centuries to entertain house guests. The entertainment usually takes place in the tea room, which is no larger than about nine square feet and contains an alcove and a small fireplace for the kettle. The guest, in order to get in the room must crawl first through a tiny entrance hall less than three feet square. Here he rinses his mouth and hands before entering the tea room.

Sake, "rice wine," is often served at the dinner table together with the meal. The warmed sake is brought to the table in a small bottle, and the guest holds his miniature cup in his right hand partly supported by the left. After his cup is filled by the hostess, the guest then pours for the next person, or the hostess. It is not considered good manners to pour for oneself.

SOUP

Next to rice, soup is the most important food for the Japanese. It is served at every meal—breakfast, lunch, and dinner. There are two kinds of soups, clear soup (SUIMONO) and soy-bean paste (MISO soup). MISO soup commonly is called breakfast soup. A simple Japanese breakfast consists of a bowl of rice, a bowl of soup, and four or five pieces of pickles. This was my favorite breakfast menu when I was a student in Tokyo. It cost me at that time 10 Sen (two and a half cents in American money).

Clear soup is served at lunch and dinner, usually first, but sometimes, when there are many dishes, at the end of the meal with rice. The Japanese formerly ate soup by using chopsticks for the vegetables, fish, or meat in the soup and then drinking the stock like tea. Nowadays they use spoons.

❦ DASHI (SOUP STOCK)

All Japanese soups are based on a soup stock called DASHI. Pure Japanese DASHI is made of KONBU (dried seaweed tangle), and KATSUOBUSHI (shredded dried bonito). Ready-made DASHI is also available in markets carrying Oriental foods. It is called "soup-no-moto" and comes in pow-

123

dered form, easy to mix with water. If these foods are not available in your area, chicken bouillon cubes may be substituted.

5 cups water	½ cup *katsuobushi* shavings
1 square inch seaweed tangle	(bonito)
(*konbu*)	¼ teaspoon monosodium glutamate

1. Put seaweed tangle in saucepan with 5 cups water. Heat to a point just before boiling, when large bubbles begin to appear, then take out the tangle and discard or flavor will be too strong.

2. Add *katsuobushi*, bring to a boiling point, and turn off fire. Let stand 5 minutes. When the *katsuobushi* sinks, strain into another saucepan. Discard the *katsuobushi*.

NOTE: It is perfectly all right to make *dashi* ahead of time. It will keep several days in jars in the refrigerator.

Japanese soups are divided into two kinds, thick and clear, both based on DASHI.

MISO *soup is a thick soup, made of a paste from the yellow soy bean. There are two kinds of* MISO:

1. SHIRO MISO, *called white* MISO, *actually yellow in color, and*

2. AKAMISO, *called red* MISO, *which is brown in color.*

To make MISO *the soy beans are cooked and mashed in a long process, but one can buy already-made* MISO *at a Japanese grocery.* MISO *soup may be made with any mixture of meat, fish, vegetables, or* tofu *(bean curd cake). This is the common Japanese breakfast for all classes.*

The Japanese clear soup is a company soup used at lunch or dinner.

124

It is made with the DASHI *stock and meat or fish and vegetables, flavored with a dash of pepper, salt, soy sauce, wine and monosodium glutamate.*

❧ JAPANESE SOUP (MISO SHIRU)

1 quart *dashi* (*see page 123*)
½ cup *shiro miso*
2 green onions, chopped

½ *tofu* (bean curd cake) cut into
½ inch cubes
½ teaspoon monosodium glutamate

1. Heat *dashi* (soup stock) until very hot, add *miso* and stir until *miso* is dissolved, then bring to a boil. This will make a medium thick soup.

2. Add cubed *tofu* and green onions and remove from heat. Do not keep on boiling after the *tofu* is added.

3. Add monosodium glutamate and serve hot. Serves 6 persons.

NOTE: Any vegetable—spinach, *dai-kon* (Japanese radish), turnips, carrots, celery, etc.—may be added to this soup. Put vegetables in soup after *miso* is dissolved, cook about 5 minutes before adding *tofu*.

❧ CHICKEN MEAT BALL SOUP (TORINIKU-NO-SUMASHI)

Delicious company soup.

½ pound chicken
1 egg white
2 teaspoons cornstarch
2 teaspoons salt
5 tablespoons cooked green peas
4 to 5 cups *dashi* (*see page 123*)

1 teaspoon salt
2 tablespoons soy sauce
½ teaspoon monosodium glutamate
1 green onion, chopped
5 slices lemon peel

1. Grind or chop chicken finely, add egg white, cornstarch, salt, and green peas. Mix well and divide into 10 little meat balls.

2. Steam meat balls for about 10 minutes.

3. Boil *dashi* (soup stock), add salt, soy sauce, and monosodium glutamate for seasoning.

4. Put chicken meat balls, chopped green onions, and sliced lemon peel into individual soup bowls.

5. Pour boiled soup in each bowl and serve hot.

6. Enough for 5 servings. Serves 5-6 persons.

❦ CLAM SOUP (HAMAGURI SHIRU)

12 clams with shells	1 teaspoon to 1 tablespoon of salt
4½ cups hot water	½ tablespoon lemon peel,
½ to 1 tablespoon soy sauce	thinly sliced
1 tablespoon dry white wine	

1. Soak clams in cold water and clean the sand out. Wash very thoroughly.

2. Put clams in a saucepan, cover with water and bring to a boil.

3. When the shells open, season with wine, soy sauce and salt to taste; reduce heat and keep warm until serving.

4. Before serving, put sliced lemon peels and several clams in each bowl, then pour in soup. Serves 5-6 persons.

NOTE: Clams have some salt in them, so don't use too much salt.

FISH AND SEA FOOD

JAPAN *is an island country and therefore marine products have been among the important foods for the Japanese for centuries, and they cannot imagine a truly Japanese dinner without fish or shellfish. Naturally, the art of cooking fish has been well developed in Japan. Among the many fish dishes,* SASHIMI *(raw fish) is the most famous. I hear my American friends say often, "How could you think of eating raw fish?" I used to think so too, and I did not touch* SASHIMI *when it was served. But once you taste it and get used to it, you consider no meal complete without it. So let us start out with the* SASHIMI *recipe first.*

❧ SLICED RAW FISH (SASHIMI)

SASHIMI *is a thin-sliced raw fish treat, usually served immediately after the soup.* SAKE *is usually served with* SASHIMI*. It is most important that the fish be very fresh. Many kinds of fish can be used to make* SASHIMI*. Bonito is perhaps the best and most popular but any tender white fish local to your area can be used. Also favorites of the Japanese are lobster and abalone* SASHIMI*. These must first be dipped into boiling water for only a second. If left in boiling water they will become tough.*

1 fresh white fish	Japanese horseradish
Soy sauce	(*wasabi*) canned
Mirin (Japanese sweet rice wine)	Shredded *dai-kon* or carrots

127

1. Slice fish very thin into small serving pieces, ½ by ½ inches or so.

2. Place attractively on serving dish either beside or over the shredded vegetables. Also put horseradish on the serving dish beside the fish.

3. Serve each person a small dish of mixed soy sauce and *mirin*. He may then add as much or as little horseradish to this mixture as he wishes. Dip fish slice into sauce and eat. Serves 4 persons.

❧ TEMPURA (DEEP-FRIED FISH OR VEGETABLES)

TEMPURA *is food deep-fried in oil after being dipped in a mixture of egg, water and flour. This is the Japanese equivalent of the American southern fried style.* TEMPURA *is a well-developed Japanese cooking technique. The secret of delicious* TEMPURA *is the harmony of four elements —fresh ingredients, light coating, nice-smelling cooking oil, and a tasty sauce.*

Fried shrimp or lobster is typical. But vegetables, such as leeks, carrots, eggplants, green onions, and green peppers can also be fried. You can slice the vegetables any shape you like; diagonal thin slices are popular. Vegetables called KARA-AGE *are fried lightly with little oil and without coatings. Fried dishes are more tasty when hot.*

❧ TEMPURA NUMBER 1 (FRIED SHRIMP)

1 pound prawns (large shrimp)   2 cups vegetable oil for deep frying

BATTER:

1 egg   1 cup flour
1 cup water   Dash of salt

128

1. Remove shells from prawns, leaving the tails on to be used as handles for dipping. Cut through the back (outside curve) with a sharp knife about ⅓ of the way. Then cut along the back about halfway through and spread open to butterfly shape. Remove entrails (the black streak) from the back. Wash and drain very thoroughly.

2. Prepare batter by mixing water and egg, then add flour and salt gradually. This is best done with a wire egg beater. Do not mix too much. Chill batter at least one hour before using.

3. Heat oil to about 350° in a deep frypan. The oil should be at least 2 inches deep. This may be done at the table if you have an electric deep fat frying pan.

4. Fry only 5 or 6 prawns at a time. This prevents cooling the oil too much.

5. Take the prawn by the tail, dip it through the batter, and drop into the heated oil. Fry about 5 minutes, turning once to brown both sides. When the prawns turn light brown, take them out.

6. Serve shrimp with one or both sauces on the next page. Serves 5-6 persons.

NOTE: Any type of vegetable may be batter-fried and served with the shrimps. For example: dry onion rings, carrots, string beans, green pepper strips. Cut all vegetables into thin strips.

❧ TEMPURA NUMBER 2 (FRIED SHRIMP)

This batter will be soft; not as crisp as Tempura Number 1.

1 pound prawns (large shrimp)   Any type of oil for deep frying
leaving on tails

BATTER:

1 cup flour	½ teaspoon ginger
1 teaspoon sugar	2 eggs, unbeaten
1 teaspoon salt	½ cup milk or ¾ cup water

1. Prepare prawns as in Tempura Number 1.

2. Mix milk and eggs with wire egg beater, then mix in other ingredients. Mix until smooth. (Batter will be medium thick.)

3. Holding each shrimp by its tail, dip in the batter, and deep-fry. (*see Tempura Number 1 for deep frying method.*)

4. Serve hot with one of following sauces. Serves 5-6 persons.

❦ TEMPURA DIP

½ cup water or soup stock	1 tablespoon sherry
½ cup soy sauce	1 teaspoon sugar

Combine all ingredients and cook about 5 minutes but do not boil. Serve with tempura.

❦ TEMPURA SAUCE

To a little catsup add a thin paste made from dry mustard and soy sauce with a little sugar and monosodium glutamate. If you wish add some sherry. Vary amounts to suit your own taste. Serve with tempura.

❦ FRIED PRAWNS (TEMPURA) ON RICE

1 cup cooked rice (hot)	½ cup *dashi* soup per serving
2 or 3 fried prawns per serving	

130

1. Cook rice (*see recipe page 62*).

2. Heat *dashi* (*see recipe page 123*).

3. Cook prawns (*Tempura Number 1, page 128*).

4. Put hot rice in rice bowls with cover. Add 2 or 3 prawns and pour about ½ cup *dashi* into each bowl. Cover and serve hot. Serves 5-6 persons.

NOTE: Egg noodles or buckwheat noodles can be substituted for rice. They are also delicious.

❧ BROILED PRAWNS (EBI-NO-MATSUKAZEYAKI)

1 pound prawns
2 to 3 tablespoons soy sauce
1 teaspoon sugar

1½ tablespoons *mirin* or sherry
1 tablespoon toasted sesame seeds

1. Clean prawns and take off shells, leaving the tails on. Take out the veins.

2. Combine soy sauce, sugar and sherry. Marinate shrimps for 15 minutes in this mixture, then remove. Drain well.

3. Thread shrimp on 2 skewers. If only one skewer is used, they will not turn easily.

4. Broil over charcoal for 3 to 5 minutes or until cooked thoroughly, or bake at 375° for 5 to 8 minutes. Baste once or twice with marinade while cooking.

5. Sprinkle with sesame seeds before serving. Serves 5-6 persons.

❧ SCALLOPS TERIYAKI (GAI-BASHI-RA-YAKI)

1 pound scallops, fresh or frozen
¼ cup brown sugar
2 tablespoons soy sauce
2 tablespoons salad oil
1 teaspoon fresh grated ginger,
or ⅛ teaspoon powdered ginger

1 clove garlic, minced
½ teaspoon salt
1 can (1 pound 4 ounces)
pineapple chunks
¼ cup pineapple juice from can

1. Wash and cut large scallops in half.

2. Combine brown sugar, soy sauce, salad oil, ginger, garlic, salt, and pineapple juice. Pour over scallops. Let stand for 5 to 10 minutes.

3. Alternating scallops and pineapple, put them on 6 skewers.

4. Place skewers across a baking pan 10" x 6" x 1". Baste with sauce.

5. Bake in 450° oven for 15 to 20 minutes; turn and baste twice while baking. Serves 5-6 persons.

NOTE: Do not overbake or scallops will not be tender. These may be served as an entrée or as hors d'oeuvre.

❧ FRIED CRAB MEAT (KANI-NO FUWA-FUWA-AGE)

¼ to ½ pound crab meat or
1 can crab meat
½ bunch spinach or 2 green onions
2 eggs

Dash of salt
1 tablespoon arrowroot or
cornstarch
Oil for deep frying

1. Flake crab meat.

2. Cut boiled spinach in 1-inch lengths or chop 2 green onions.

132

3. Separate eggs; beat egg whites, add a dash of salt. (The eggs should not be dry.) Add egg yolks, cornstarch, flaked crab and spinach to egg whites and mix thoroughly.

4. Heat oil to 375°. Drop crab mixture by tablespoonfuls into hot oil and fry about 1 minute or until light brown. Drop only 5 spoonfuls at a time to avoid cooling fat too much.

5. Serve with soy sauce mixed with prepared mustard. Serves 5-6 persons.

NOTE: May also be served with Chinese Basic Barbecue Sauce recipe (*see page 83*).

❧ SKEWERED LOBSTER (LOBSTER-NO-KUSHIYAKI)

4 small frozen lobster tails (about 8 ounces each)	1 teaspoon grated ginger root or ¼ teaspoon ginger powder
¼ cup salad oil	2 teaspoons sugar
2 tablespoons soy sauce	1 clove garlic minced
1 tablespoon onion, minced	1 teaspoon pepper
1 teaspoon salt	½ teaspoon monosodium glutamate
1 teaspoon dry mustard	

1. Cook lobster tails in salted boiling water for 2 or 3 minutes.

2. Combine remaining ingredients; marinate lobster tails 3 to 4 hours. Turn several times to marinate evenly.

3. Thread lobster tails on individual skewers.

4. Broil on charcoal, or oven broil for about 10 minutes, basting often with marinade until thoroughly heated.

5. Serve plain or with hot sauce (*see page 85*). Serves 4 persons.

❧ FISH TERIYAKI

5 or 6 pieces sliced salmon, tuna, rockfish, or mackerel

SAUCE:

¾ cup soy sauce
¾ cup sugar
¼ cup sake or sherry

½ teaspoon monosodium glutamate
(optional)

1. Prepare sauce by mixing soy sauce, sugar, wine and monosodium glutamate.

2. Cut fish into small steak-size pieces and marinate about 30 minutes in sauce.

3. Remove the fish from marinade and place in hot broiler. Broil one side about 4 minutes, then turn and broil other side about 6 minutes.

4. While broiling, baste about three times with sauce.

5. When nicely browned, serve hot, sprinkled with a little of the warmed sauce. Serves 5-6 persons.

Or sprinkle a very little salt on both sides of the fish, and broil on both sides until brown. While broiling, baste about three times with sauce.

NOTE: Broil these over charcoal, frying-pan, or in an oven.

MEAT DISHES

THE JAPANESE *are not great meat eaters. In early days, cows and horses were forbidden food because they were employed in cultivating farm land and considered important farm implements, and during the eighth century (Nara period) when Buddhism flourished, the Japanese were discouraged from eating meat for religious reasons.*

But now one of the most popular Japanese dishes is SUKIYAKI. *The word means plough-roasted, or roasted on the plough. It seems that* SUKI-YAKI *was influenced by the Korean* JUHN KOL *dish, and about the middle of the nineteenth century* SUKIYAKI *became popular with the Japanese.*

When SUKIYAKI *is served, it is customary for the guests to sit on cushions on a straw-matted floor, cross-legged, around a low, round table. In the middle of this table is either an electric heater or small gas stove, or, in the pure Japanese style, a traditional charcoal-cooking brazier. The saucepan or cooking utensil rests on top of the brazier. The guests and host sit around the table while the waitress or maid is putting the ingredients into the saucepan, and wait for the ingredients to boil. Usually each individual takes from the saucepan what he wants, but sometimes the maid or host (if there is no maid) serves. Characteristic of* SUKIYAKI *is that you watch it cooking (sometimes you cook it yourself), eat it hot, and enjoy a happy family atmosphere, sitting around a low dining table. There are many kinds of* SUKIYAKI. TOKYO SUKIYAKI *is the best known, but you will also enjoy* MIZU-TAKI, *similar to* SUKIYAKI, *which has become popular on the West Coast, especially in the San Francisco Bay area. Beef is used for all these dishes.*

❧ SUKIYAKI (TOKYO STANDARD)

½ pound tenderloin beef,
  sliced bacon-thin
2 medium onions, thinly sliced
1 bunch green onions, cut
  diagonally (include green tops)
½ cup fresh mushrooms, sliced
½ cup sliced bamboo shoots

½ bunch watercress, cut leaves
  in half (optional)
½ pound fresh spinach, cut in
  2 inch pieces
1 *tofu* (bean curd cake) if desired
½ pound yam noodles (*shiratake*
  or *itogonyaku*) (optional)

SEASONING:

½ cup (or less) of soy sauce
2 tablespoons sherry or white wine

½ cup water or *dashi*
4 tablespoons sugar

1. Have butcher slice beef for you if possible. Ask for *sukiyaki*-sliced tenderloin.

2. Slice all vegetables and arrange attractively with meat on a large platter.

3. Combine ingredients with seasoning sauce. Put in attractive bowl.

4. Cooking is usually done at the table. The typical Japanese way of cooking is in a round shallow pan without handles over a *hibachi*. An electric frying pan is a simple substitute for the American home.

5. Place a piece of beef suet in the hot skillet and melt; put one-third of the meat into the pan. Brown meat pieces on both sides and pour half of the sauce over this.

136

6. Push the cooked beef to one corner of the skillet, add about ⅓ of the vegetables and *tofu*, and cook about 5 or 6 minutes. Then serve with hot rice.

7. Repeat in similar manner for second and third servings. Cook meat by quickly simmering in the leftover sauce in pan as it cannot be browned at this time. This manner of cooking small amounts frequently during a meal assures fresh, crisp, hot foods throughout the dinner. Serves 4 persons.

NOTE: If desired, beat raw egg in a small bowl and dip the *sukiyaki* before eating. It is delicious and nutritious. *Sukiyaki* is enhanced if served with a dinner wine or *sake*.

♨ MIZU-TAKI

THIS IS *a typical Japanese* MIZU-TAKI *recipe and in reality is a simplified version of* SUKIYAKI. *It should be cooked at the table in a manner similar to* SUKIYAKI—*in a frying pan, chafing dish, or the Korean* SIN SUL LO. *The major difference between the two dishes is that* SUKIYAKI *is cooked in a flavored sauce while* MIZU-TAKI *is cooked without a sauce. It is then dipped into a special sauce, a bite at a time, while being eaten. The typical Japanese cooker for this is a round, heavy iron frypan without handles called* SUKIYAKI NABE. *This is traditionally a winter-time dish.*

½ pound prime rib or beef sirloin, sliced thin
¼ pound fresh mushrooms, sliced in half
½ to 1 bunch green onions, sliced in 2-inch lengths
1 small can sliced bamboo shoots
½ bunch young, tender spinach leaves, stems removed
1 *tofu* (bean curd) cubed
3 cups water or chicken broth

137

SAUCE: *Mix together*

1 cup soy sauce	1 teaspoon sugar
Juice of one lime	1 teaspoon monosodium glutamate

1. Have butcher *sukiyaki*-cut beef for you if possible.

2. Arrange the meat and vegetables very attractively on a large tray or platter.

3. Heat water or chicken broth in skillet or chafing dish at the table. When the liquid is barely bubbling, add half of thin sliced beef, mushrooms, spinach, bamboo shoots, green onion and *tofu*.

4. Mix sauce ingredients and serve in individual bowls.

5. When meat and vegetable tidbits are cooked, each person lifts out what he desires and dips them into the sauce.

6. Serve with hot rice. Serves 4 persons.

NOTE: *Mizu-taki* may also be made with thin sliced chicken or pork. Although not authentic, some Western tastes might prefer the red sauce as a dip instead of the above recipe (*see page 85*).

❧ MIZU-TAKI (DELUXE)

1 pound lean beef, sliced thin	½ can bamboo shoots
1 pound spinach	1 bunch green onions
1 bunch Chinese cabbage	1 or 2 carrots
2 medium onions	1 or 2 celery stalks cut diagonally
1 egg plant (optional)	1 *tofu* (bean curd) optional
¼ pound fresh mushrooms	

138

1. Scrape carrots and cut into flower shape. Wash Chinese cabbage and cut into ½-inch pieces. Wash mushrooms and slice. Wash egg plant, quarter, and slice. Cut onions in half and slice thin. Cut green onions into 2-inch pieces. Put all vegetables aside.

2. Cut sirloin beef into strips about 3 by 6 inches. (When purchasing beef, ask the butcher to slice bacon-thin.)

3. Put about 2 cups of cold water in frying pan and bring to a rapid boil. Put meat slices in and let cook for about 5 minutes and put in vegetables and *tofu*. Cook over high flame for about 10 minutes and then continue cooking over medium flame for about 5 minutes.

4. Serve in bowls. Put sauce in separate dish for dipping. Serve rice in separate bowl. Serves 4 persons.

❦ MIZU-TAKI SAUCE NUMBER 1 (SESAME SEED SAUCE)

½ cup sesame seeds
½ cup soy sauce
2 tablespoons vinegar or
  lemon juice

¾ cup broth or water
1 clove garlic or ginger
Sugar
Monosodium glutamate

Toast sesame seeds. Put all ingredients in blender and mix.

❦ MIZU-TAKI SAUCE NUMBER 2 (PEANUT SAUCE)

½ cup chunk-style peanut butter
1½ tablespoons soy sauce
1 tablespoon water
½ teaspoon sugar

2 or 3 drops Tabasco sauce
1 clove garlic, minced
½ cup water

Put all ingredients in blender and mix.

❧ CHICKEN, SHRIMPS AND VEGETABLES (YOSE-NABE)

This dish is similar to sukiyaki and should be fixed at the table.

½ pound raw chicken breasts sliced
½ pound shelled shrimps or 1 can
  shrimps
¼ pound mushrooms, sliced
  in quarters
1 carrot, thinly sliced
1 can sliced bamboo shoots
¼ pound fresh, young sugar peas
  (China peas in pod)

2 to 3 cups chicken stock or
  2 cubes chicken bouillon
  dissolved in hot water
¼ teaspoon salt
1 or 2 tablespoons soy sauce
1 tablespoon sugar
1 tablespoon white wine or sherry

1. Slice chicken breast thinly. Slice mushrooms and carrots. Cut off ends of sugar peas but leave whole.

2. Arrange all ingredients very attractively on a large platter. (This may be done in advance of dinner and set in the refrigerator.)

3. First put into the skillet all of the stock, salt, soy sauce, sugar, and wine. Bring to boil, then add ½ of chicken, shrimps, and vegetables and cook 4 to 5 minutes. Serve with hot rice.

4. Add remaining parts of ingredients little by little as needed. Serves 4 persons.

❧ BEEF TERIYAKI

BROILED *dishes such as this and the following pork dishes are usually cooked over a charcoal fire on a gridiron or spit on a skewer. An oven can be used for broiling, but charcoal fire is better.*

1 pound tenderloin steak or club steak

TERIYAKI SAUCE:

1 to 2 tablespoons soy sauce
2 tablespoons sugar
½ teaspoon grated fresh ginger or
   ¼ teaspoon powdered ginger

1 clove garlic, minced
2 tablespoons wine, sherry
  or burgundy
2 tablespoons salad oil

1. Cut steak against grain into thin strips about 2 inches wide.

2. Mix *teriyaki* sauce and pour over steak.

3. Marinate for at least an hour.

4. Drain steak and fry quickly in a heavy, very hot, skillet with butter or oil.

5. Serve at once with any desired vegetable. Serves 2 persons.

🌱 PORK TERIYAKI

THE JAPANESE *do not eat much pork. I do not know why—perhaps because they have concentrated on sea food, of which they have such an abundant supply, and neglected raising pigs as domestic animals.*

1 pound pork shoulder, cut into
  2 inch cubes
¼ cup soy sauce
2 tablespoons sugar
1 clove garlic, minced

½ teaspoon fresh grated ginger
  or dash ginger powder
½ teaspoon monosodium glutamate
1 tablespoon toasted sesame seeds
  (for garnish)

1. Mix soy sauce, sugar, garlic, and ginger.

2. Marinate pork cubes in the above sauce for at least 2 to 3 hours.

3. Broil over a slow charcoal fire for about 30 minutes or until golden

brown on both sides (use skewers) or bake or broil in oven at 350 degrees for 45 minutes or until well done. While broiling the meat turn occasionally.

4. Garnish with sesame seeds. Serves 2 persons.

❧ PORK WITH VEGETABLES (UMANI)

½ pound lean pork, cut into
  ½ inch cubes
1 cup water
1 cup carrots, diced
1 small can bamboo shoots,
  cut into small pieces
½ pound green beans, cut
  2 inches long

1 small can (5 ounces) water
  chestnuts, cut into halves
1 can mushrooms or Oriental
  mushrooms sliced
2 tablespoons soy sauce
1 teaspoon sugar
1 teaspoon monosodium glutamate

1. Preheat large saucepan; put pork in; add water and cover. Bring to boil, remove cover, and skim scum off from surface of water. Simmer covered and cook about 20 minutes or until meat is almost tender.

2. Add carrots, bamboo shoots, green beans, water chestnuts, and mushrooms. Cook about 10 minutes.

3. Then add soy sauce, sugar, monosodium glutamate; bring to boil and simmer until vegetables are tender.

4. Serve with cooked rice. Serves 5-6 persons.

CHICKEN AND EGG DISHES

BOILED FOOD *is called* NINIMONO, *and resembles food served Cape Cod style. Popular are boiled shrimp and bamboo shoots, boiled chicken, vegetables, and eggs. Fresh materials should be used and boiled quickly to keep the flavor.*

Japanese use cooked rice in various ways as the principal part of each dish; OYAKO-DOMBURI *and* TAMAGO-DOMBURI *are dishes in which chicken, eggs, and vegetables are combined. These dishes are simple and economical, but tasty. They are also time-saving dishes.*

❧ BOILED CHICKEN AND VEGETABLES (NIMONO)

1 to 2 pounds frying chicken, cut into serving pieces
6 cups water
2 teaspoons salt
1 to 2 tablespoons soy sauce
2 teaspoons or more sugar
1 teaspoon monosodium glutamate
2 or 3 carrots
3 or 4 Oriental dried mushrooms
¼ pound or less sugar peas
1 can bamboo shoots

1. Bring to boil 6 cups water. Add to chicken and cook about 40 minutes over a low flame or until chicken is tender. Skim several times while cooking.

2. Add 2 teaspoons salt, 1 tablespoon soy sauce, sugar, and monosodium glutamate and cook another 10 minutes.

3. Slice the carrots into rounds and cut the edges into flower shapes.

4. Soak the dried mushrooms in warm water until soft, then remove the stems.

5. String the sugar peas and cut the ends so that all are the same length. Drop the peas into salted, boiling water and parboil. Drain well.

6. Put the soup stock into a large pan. Add the mushrooms, carrots, and bamboo shoots. Cook until tender. Just before removing from flame, add the peas.

7. Arrange the chicken and vegetables attractively on a large plate or individual plates. Thicken the remaining soup with cornstarch. Pour the gravy over the meat and vegetables.

8. Serve while hot with rice. Serves 6 persons.

❦ STEAMED EGGS AND VEGETABLES (CHAWAN-MUSHI)

½ cup cooked chicken, finely cut
½ can of cooked small shrimps
2 bamboo shoots, sliced
½ cup cooked peas or cooked spinach
1 can mushrooms or Oriental dried mushrooms, sliced

4 eggs slightly beaten
1 tablespoon soy sauce
4 cups stock (2 cubes of chicken bouillon dissolved in hot water)
2 teaspoons sugar
Salt to taste
½ teaspoon monosodium glutamate

It is necessary to have a pot for steam-cooking and individual covered dishes.

144

1. Divide chicken, shrimps, and vegetables equally in 4 to 5 bowls. If dry mushrooms are used, soak in warm water 15 minutes or more before slicing.

2. Beat eggs and mix with bouillon stock. Add sugar, salt and monosodium glutamate.

3. Pour egg and stock mixture over the ingredients in the bowls.

4. Cover each bowl and cook in the hot steaming pot for 15 to 20 minutes. Egg mixture will not be smooth like velvet if too high heat is used; keep water at simmer. Serves 5-6 persons.

❧ RICE WITH CHICKEN AND EGGS (OYAKO-DOMBURI)

4 to 5 cups cooked rice
1 cup *dashi* or chicken bouillon
3 or 4 tablespoons soy sauce
3 tablespoons sherry
½ cup raw chicken breast,
 sliced thinly
1 onion sliced lengthwise

¼ to ½ pound fresh mushrooms,
 sliced thinly
5 eggs
1 teaspoon monosodium glutamate
Green onions, chopped,
 for garnish

1. Cook rice (*see page 62*).

2. Bring *dashi* or bouillon to boil, add soy sauce, sherry, chicken, onion and mushrooms. Cook uncovered for about 5 minutes or until chicken is tender.

3. Divide the hot rice into 4 or 5 rice bowls with covers.

4. Put the *dashi* mixture into a frying pan over low heat.

5. Beat eggs lightly and add to the mixture in the frying pan and stir just a little. Add monosodium glutamate.

6. When egg is half cooked, pour over hot rice in the bowls, garnish with green onions and cover. Serve immediately. Serves 5-6 persons.

NOTE: This is delicious and very light. If possible serve in covered bowls to preserve heat.

❧ RICE WITH EGGS (TAMAGO-DOMBURI)

This is similar to OYAKO-DOMBURI. *The same method is used, omitting chicken.*

4 to 5 cups cooked rice
2 cups *dashi* (*see page 123*)
  or 2 chicken bouillon cubes
  dissolved in hot water
7 eggs
2 stalks green onion,
  sliced diagonally

1 teaspoon sugar
1 teaspoon monosodium glutamate
3 or 4 tablespoons soy sauce
2 teaspoons salt
2 or 3 tablespoons sherry

1. Cook rice (*see page 62*).

2. Bring *dashi* or bouillon to boil. Add soy sauce, sherry, sugar, monosodium glutamate, salt and green onion. Cook about 1 minute.

3. Add lightly beaten eggs, cover, and cook another minute or two.

4. When eggs are half cooked, pour the mixture over hot rice, which has been divided into 4 or 5 individual bowls. Cover and serve hot. Serves 5-6 persons.

146

SALADS

Although the Japanese *are great vegetable eaters, they have not developed salad dishes as Westerners understand them.* Tsukemono *(pickled vegetables) and* sunomono *(vinegar vegetables) are the typical Japanese "salads." Both are cooked in advance and are served before (as hors d'oeuvre with sake) during or after the final course. They are salty and served as appetizers. The Japanese call them* okazu, *(side dishes). I have selected two each of such recipes. You can find* takuan *(pickled radish) in any Japanese grocery store in this country.*

❧ CAULIFLOWER SALAD WITH WALNUTS (HANA-CABBAGE)

1 head cauliflower, cut into small serving pieces	1 teaspoon sugar
½ cup or less of walnuts	4 teaspoons vinegar
2 teaspoons salt	Dash of pepper
	1 cup of water

1. Bring water to boil in a saucepan. Add 1 teaspoon salt and cook the cauliflower about 5 minutes or until tender, drain well.

2. Chop walnuts finely, and lightly brown them in a frying pan.

3. Use meat grinder or electric blender to grind the nuts fine (almost to a paste), then add 1 teaspoon salt, sugar, vinegar and a dash of pepper.

147

4. Mix the cauliflower and walnut paste very gently and serve cold, but do not chill. Serves 4 persons.

❦ CUCUMBER SALAD (KYURI-MOMI)

1 cucumber, sliced	Dash monosodium glutamate
1 teaspoon salt	1 green onion top, chopped
1 teaspoon sugar	1 teaspoon toasted sesame seeds
1 teaspoon vinegar	Dash soy sauce

1. Do not peel cucumber unless skin is tough. Wash and cut in half lengthwise. Scoop out most of the seeds. Slice diagonally paper thin.

2. Place cucumber in bowl, sprinkle with salt, and let stand about 15 to 20 minutes.

3. Mix well and squeeze tightly between palms of hands and let all the juice drain out.

4. Add sugar, vinegar, and monosodium glutamate and chill thoroughly.

5. Serve on individual plates, garnished with green onion tops, sesame seeds, and a small dash of soy sauce. Serves 2 persons.

❦ VEGETABLES WITH VINEGAR DRESSING (SUNOMONO)

1 or 2 cucumbers	½ pound bean sprouts
6 radishes	

VINEGAR DRESSING:

4 tablespoons vinegar	⅛ teaspoon salt
1 tablespoon soy sauce	¼ teaspoon monosodium glutamate
2 teaspoons sugar	

148

1. Parboil bean sprouts and then drain. Let cool.

2. Pare cucumber and cut lengthwise, then slice diagonally. Sprinkle on salt lightly. Let stand for about 10 minutes. Press all the water out.

3. Wash the radishes, then slice very thinly.

4. Combine the bean sprouts, cucumbers, and radishes. Arrange attractively in a medium-size bowl or in individual bowls.

5. Mix the vinegar-dressing well. Pour over the vegetables and serve immediately. Serves 5-6 persons.

❧ SPINACH WITH SESAME SEED DRESSING (AEMONO)

1 pound spinach	3 tablespoons sesame seeds or
Water	black sesame seeds
Salt	½ teaspoon sugar
1 tablespoon soy sauce	Dash of monosodium glutamate

1. Wash spinach thoroughly. Boil water, then put in spinach and 1 teaspoon of salt. Boil for 1 minute (do not overcook), drain and let cool.

2. Heat frypan over medium flame, and then add the sesame seeds and toast them until they are light brown. Grind either in an electric blender or meat grinder.

3. Add soy sauce, sugar, and monosodium glutamate to sesame seeds.

4. Cut the spinach into 1½ inch lengths, press the water out.

5. Mix gently with the ground sesame seed dressing; serve in a small bowl. Serves 5-6 persons.

NOTE: Typical Japanese way of grinding sesame seeds is in a *suribachi* (earthenware mortar).

149

DESSERTS

THE RICH VARIETY *of desserts, including Westernized pies, cakes, and ice creams, are available in the modern restaurants in all major Japanese cities. The traditional Japanese cakes called* O-KASHI *are made from rice, red beans, agar-agar or gelatine, rice or corn flour, eggs, millet jelly, and sugar. Fresh fruits and rice cake (*O-SEMBEI*) are also served as desserts. Most Japanese desserts are very sweet. Tea is usually served with dessert. I am introducing three recipes that should go well with any Japanese dish in this book, and for which the materials are easily found in neighborhood grocery stores.*

❦ JAPANESE DESSERT (MITSUMAME)

Kanten, an unflavored gelatine made from agar-agar
Fresh fruits in season: strawberries, bananas, apples, oranges, pineapple or canned fruit cocktail

1 tablespoon sherry
Toasted almonds for topping
1 cup water
1 cup sugar

1. Break *kanten* into 2 or 3 pieces. Soak in a pan of water for an hour or more. Remove *kanten* from the pan; squeeze out the water.

150

2. Break the softened *kanten* into very small pieces; add 2 to 2½ cups water per each original *kanten*.

3. Cook and boil until *kanten* pieces dissolve and water becomes smooth.

4. Filter with a very fine cheesecloth. Add a little salt or lemon juice.

5. Pour into a shallow pan and chill in refrigerator until set.

6. Boil sugar and water until sugar dissolves. Cool. Maple syrup may be substituted for sugar syrup.

7. After the *kanten* has thickened cut in ½-inch cubes. Put some *kanten* and any desired fruits or fruit cocktail in a glass dish. Mix syrup with sherry and pour over the top and sprinkle with toasted almonds. Serves 5-6 persons.

NOTE: Unflavored gelatine may be substituted for *kanten*; the flavor will be just slightly different, texture and appearance will be the same, and preparation time much less. Food coloring can be used to tint the *kanten* or gelatine. Also you can buy pink-colored *kanten*.

SHOPPING GUIDE FOR ORIENTAL INGREDIENTS

The following may be purchased in any Chinese or Japanese grocery store. Most of these items can also be found in super-markets:

Almond cookies
Bamboo shoots
Bean curds
Bean thread noodles
Chinese black beans
Chinese greens { Bok Choy / Cabbage / Parsley
Dai-kon (radish)
Dashi-no-moto (soup stock)
Dried mushrooms

Five fragances powder
Fortune cookies
Fried noodles
Ginger roots
Japanese pickles (Takuan)
Kamaboku (Japanese mold of steamed fish)
Kanten (agar agar)
Konbu (Japanese seaweed tangle)
Miso (Japanese bean paste)

Mirin (Japanese sweet wine)
Monosodium glutamate (Acc'ent or ajinomoto)
Plum sauce
Sake (Japanese wine)
Sesame seeds
Sesame oil
Soy sauce
Water chestnuts (fresh or canned)
Won-ton skins

NOTE: In case you cannot find the above ingredients in your neighborhood markets, you could order them (or substitute as indicated in the recipes) from the following stores:

CHINESE INGREDIENTS:

Wing Song Chang Co. Inc.—1076 Stockton Street, San Francisco, California
Wing Fat Co.—35 Mott Street, New York, N.Y.
Lun Yick Co.—1339 Third Ave., Detroit, Michigan.
Sun Wah Hing Trading Co.—2246 Wentworth Ave., Chicago, Illinois
Yee Sing Chong Co.—950 Castelar Street, Los Angeles, California.

JAPANESE INGREDIENTS:

Sakai K. Company—1684 Post Street, San Francisco, California.
Oriental Food Shop—1302 Amsterdam Ave., New York, N.Y.
Katagiri & Co.—224 East 59th Street, New York, N.Y.

KOREAN INGREDIENTS:

Korean Food Production Co.—4716 South Normandie Ave., Los Angeles, Calif.

INDEX

154